THE PARROT FAMILY

THE
PARROT
FAMILY

Parakeets·Budgerigars·Cockatiels
Lovebirds·Lories·Macaws

W. de Grahl

ARCO PUBLISHING, INC.
NEW YORK

Acknowledgements

The photographs in this book have been supplied
by the following:
color: J. Kenning, and the author
black and white: W. Frank, K.A. Uder, and the
author

Published 1984 by Arco Publishing, Inc.
215 Park Avenue South, New York, NY 10003

© English Translation Ward Lock Limited 1981

© 1979 by Eugen Ulmer GmbH & Co. Stuttgart, Germany

© First published in Germany by Eugen Ulmer GmbH & Co., Stuttgart, Germany

First published in Great Britain in 1981 by Ward Lock Limited

Translated by Jane Muscroft BA

Printed in Hong Kong by Everbest Printing Co., Ltd.

Library of Congress Cataloging in Publication Data

De Grahl, W. (Wolfgang)
  The parrot family.

  Includes indexes.
  1. Parrots. I. Title.
SF473.P3D38   1984 636.6'865 83-17940
ISBN 0-668-06039-5 Hardcover Edition
IBSN 0-668-06043-3 Paperback Edition

Contents

Introduction

Parrots bring pleasure in many ways: because of their personality, their plumage, and because they are relatively easy to rear. These characteristics have won them an astonishingly large circle of admirers, which is growing year by year. The intelligence of the species is not without foundation since they have, relatively, the heaviest brain of all birds—the larger the birds, the larger is its brain in proportion to its size. For example, a Grey Parrot shows more intelligence than a Parrotlet.

Parrots can develop extraordinary capabilities. In particular, people find them attractive because of their capacity for association, which is especially good among the larger varieties. Other characteristics are inherent in them, too. Many have the gift of aural imitation, be it of words, tunes or noises, and some birds can even associate a particular purpose or meaning with a particular call. This desire to imitate can, by itself, bring so much entertainment and pleasure that the bird becomes almost one of the family. People also find the birds very attractive to watch as they perform acrobatics in their cages. Such skills are possible because they have strong gripping claws, two to the front and two pointing backwards, a tough, flexible muscular system and a wide range of mobility in their joints. Thus, whilst calmly preening itself, a parrot can hang from the roof of its cage by one toe, as though this were a thoroughly comfortable posture! On the floor though, the birds often appear very comical as they waddle forwards, rather like a duck. In many species this idiosyncratic motion is the result of an imbalance in body weight, caused by the proportions of the body in relation to the shortness of stride. Many parrots are also entertaining to watch feeding, using their feet as hands. No other bird uses its foot to carry a piece of apple, carrot or nut to its beak.

A Moluccan Cockatoo once demonstrated what seemed to be the peak of comedy and intelligence. With claws half-closed, he reached into a bowl of sunflower seeds and spooned out a huge helping which settled on the ball of his foot. He then lifted his foot to his beak and picked the seeds out one by one, thus sparing himself the labour of bending down to pick up each individual seed! One female Nyasa Lovebird took enormous pleasure in emptying a pot of games counters. She would take the coloured discs out one by one, then put them all back. Often, however, this little parrot would run to the edge of the table and throw her toy to the floor. She sat and watched with obvious pleasure as each counter fell before fetching another one.

Another of their attractive characteristics is the relative ease with which they can be tamed. They are eager for entertainment and play. There are even species which can be taught simple tricks and enjoy learning them. To illustrate this point, here is a selection of advertisements from an agricultural magazine:

Rarity! Bright red Macaw, young, hand-tamed, talks, laughs, very intelligent and educated, loves playing with children, unique colouring. Sits freely in the garden, comes to hand as soon as called, loves riding on bike handlebars, ideal for advertising a business. Complete with chromed stand. Open to offers, sale due to changing circumstances.

One African Grey—male—talking, completely tame. Alert, affectionate, particularly fond of men over forty, never shrieks, will spoil his future owner with tenderness, compliance. Wide repertoire of sounds – lips, kissing and other tendernesses, chiming clocks, drinking. Whistles, e.g., 'In Munich is a Hofbräuhaus'. A real beauty!

Baby Macaw guaranteed hand-reared, will lie on his back in strangers' arms, very gifted.

Parrot sought by TV and press, good talker. Please offer only exceptional birds.

Young tame Yellow-fronted Amazon, laughs, cries, coughs, talks, etc.

Grey Parrot, tame, does not screech or pluck its feathers, finest plumage, good talker, *offers* stating price.

Parrots know how to attract attention to themselves by the use of postures, noises or movements. Man has become a companion to them and any bird kept in isolation is exceedingly uneasy. So that every little bit of his head can be scratched, a bird will take up the most impossible stance. No contortion is too much for him as long as he can enjoy this pleasure with half-closed eyes.

The splendid colours of most of the parrot species are a further attraction. Their feathers gleam red, green, blue, yellow and all shades in between. Mother Nature was generous when she scattered her most luxuriant colours, although the dominant basic colour is green of one shade or another. The feathers of a healthy, well-reared parrot grow brighter and more beautiful year by year.

Anyone who keeps birds should concentrate his efforts as far as practicable on breeding, be that in the house or garden. The importation of parrots is becoming more difficult due to new restrictions. Environmental changes across the world are such that many species of parrot are being driven from their habitat, thus reducing their numbers considerably. Vast primeval forests and wildernesses are becoming increasingly developed; established nesting sites are being uprooted in civilization's quest for oil, minerals and other raw materials. Enthusiasts who confine themselves to keeping a single bird should be aware of these developments and of their own responsibilities in these circumstances.

Many species are easy to breed, particularly the Australian Parrakeets, and above all the Budgerigar. Parrots can be bred out of doors in a garden aviary. One can always offer successive broods for sale or exchange them with other breeders and in this way pay for the hobby, either entirely or in part. Breeding also gives you the additional advantage of being able to handle and tame a young bird right from the start.

Further interest comes from attempting to breed a species which has not previously bred in captivity, or only been bred with very little success. It was thanks to enthusiasts and breeders that science learned of many of the birds' habits and ways, since many of the species inhabit the densest forest habitat and cannot be reached for research studies.

The variety of colouring is very important with Budgerigars and other Parrakeets, as well as with Lovebirds. A skilled breeder can predict the inheritance of colour genes and he awaits each hatching with bated breath. He hopes for constantly improved colouring, perhaps for exhibition purposes. Chance can also throw up mutations which he had not expected.

All these are the added attractions that parrots have over other birds, so it is no wonder that they are such popular house guests. Parrots had been tamed as long ago as early Roman times. The following remark from those days will bring a wry smile to the face of any parrot lover: 'O unhappy Rome! What Age is this when women feed dogs upon their laps and men carry Parrots upon their arms!'

Buying and housing parrots

The purchase of a parrot must be very carefully considered, more so than for any other bird. The more conscientiously all the different questions are thought out beforehand, the less irritation and the more pleasure will be experienced later. Above all, a tame and very affectionate bird that has really settled down in the family cannot simply be passed on to another home.

Cost and characteristics of the birds

One important consideration is, of course, the purchase price. Greys, Amazons and some Parrakeets are the most talented imitators. Cockatoos have the most lovable disposition and can learn a variety of tricks. The easiest to breed, however, are to be found among the Australian Parrakeets, Lovebirds, Parrotlets and several others.

One must also take into account the voices of the species since, although some are negligible, others can be extremely powerful. There are also species which only make a twittering noise.

The prospective purchaser must be clear about what features he is looking for. A single bird will be quickest to grow tame and calm and ready to begin imitating.

Indoor and outdoor housing

Before deciding to keep a bird indoors, careful consideration must be given to space: you cannot keep a bird in any spare corner. The area must *not* receive full sunlight on a summer's day, be near the heating nor be in a draught. No bird cage should ever be placed on top of a television set because birds are astonishingly sensitive to vibration, and any machine in use vibrates constantly. Although radiation scientists have not yet proved that emissions from television sets are harmful to pets, the supposition that they could prove harmful in the long run has not yet been disproved. Therefore, one should on no account put a bird in the close vicinity of a television set.

The cage must always stay in the same place because the bird gets very used to it and is disturbed by any relocation. Tame parrots may remain silent for weeks after a move, until they have adjusted to the new outlook.

One must also consider the temperature factor before buying a bird. Newly imported birds should first be kept at room temperature, but never right next to a source of heat.

Cages for the larger parrots are not cheap. However, good secondhand ones can sometimes be obtained at favourable prices.

If you are thinking of keeping a bird in the garden, remember that in summer the day begins very early. Not every neighbour is a bird lover who welcomes the sound of parrots at dawn!

You must decide if your aviary is to be heated in winter. It is according to this factor that the choice of birds is made, as not all parrots can tolerate heavy frosts. However, Australian Parrakeets can, because they have been bred here for many generations and have become fully acclimatized.

A wooden aviary can only be used for those types which do not destroy wood. Some parrots' beaks can develop great strength and it is child's play for them to gnaw their way through a roofing slat. If you want to avoid continual problems, including the possibility of escape, with such a bird, a wholly metal structure is advisable.

It is not always necessary for a large bird to have a large area. There are species that make only little use of their wings, if any, and these are the ones that need branches for climbing (Amazons, Macaws, Eclectus Parrots, etc.).

Housing alternatives

Cage

Do not take it for granted that every ready-made cage is good and practical, for they are not always the result of the maker's own experience. Fashion also plays a part here. Some decorative cages are expensive and extremely impractical. Rounded cage shapes are not ideal, as they provide nothing to climb on; they can be used, however, for birds which are often let out. Such a cage should not be made of thick white rods because all that the bird inside sees is a wall of whiteness. Unfortunately, cages like this are frequently bought by beginners because they look so pleasantly modern. It is very useful if a parrot cage has horizontal bars. Almost every parrot climbs with the aid of his beak and finds it very difficult to hold on to vertical rods.

The living space for a pet can never be too big, but it can very easily be too small. Every bird needs enough space to be able to preen and fluff out its feathers. Parrots with long tails soon become unattractive to look at when kept in confined spaces. With cages for large birds, special care must be taken to ensure that the door catch is secure and the feeders are firmly anchored. It is incredible how much patience and skill a bird can put into opening what was thought to be a fool-proof fastening. The bowls, too, must be of very stout porcelain.

11

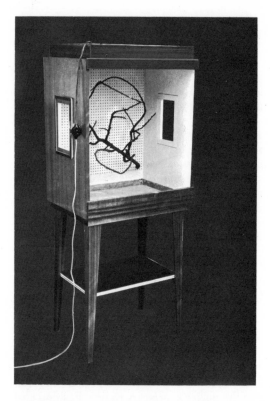

Glass-fronted cage for Parrotlets or Lovebirds.

As a rule, a floor grating is not to be recommended. Most birds cannot walk on it, and in any case the droppings usually stick to it. A layer of sand is necessary, both for hygienic and dietary reasons. The tiny grains of sand are eaten while they are still fresh, thus providing vital minerals.

Most shops stock brass-plated cages. Chromium-plated cages are very much more expensive. Plastic has taken a firm hold on cage manufacture. Usually the bars of the cages are coated with it and the bath and tray are moulded in it for small species, such as Budgerigars. In the case of cages for larger parrots, the accessories and sometimes the tray and base are made of plastic. It is a very light material which is easy to clean, and it does away with fragile panes of glass and heavy, gloomy zinc sheeting. Only the bigger cages, for large birds, have kept these because these big birds can easily bite through plastic.

For breeding, or housing smaller birds, there are plastic cages up to 70 cm (2 ft 9 in) in length. They also have plastic baths, and the bars are brass coated.

A leg chain is not advisable as it restricts the leg.

Stands, perches and climbing trees

A stand is useful for some of the tame larger species, especially for Macaws, Cockatoos and Amazons. Some birds prefer it primarily for daytime use, spending the nights in their cages. Not every new parrot will adjust to a stand; some take months to get used to it and there will certainly be others which will never take to it. The breeder must go by his own instincts in deciding when to introduce the stand as a daytime perch.

I must mention chains, although I do not recommend them. You can attach the bird to a stand, as zoos often do, with a chain that has one or two swivels to prevent it getting wound up. One end is fixed to the crossbar and the other to the bird's leg. If the chain is too fine the bird will bite it through, but if it is too thick it will overload him and become a form of torture. You will also have to change the size of the ring on the bird's leg every few months, otherwise it will look like the one in the picture above.

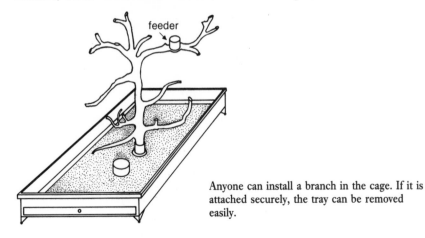

feeder

Anyone can install a branch in the cage. If it is attached securely, the tray can be removed easily.

13

Metal stands are the most practical, of course, and are proof against even the strongest beak. On the other hand, you could easily make a wooden one yourself.

A natural tree branch must be firmly fixed to a base. Its size and height are matters of personal choice. Naturally, birds will enjoy stripping the bark off it and perhaps will even eat the twigs. This can only be good for them. Renew the branch whenever necessary.

Perches are more often used in zoos. They can be unhooked, and then hung back at night. Most of the birds are also chained, but you do see parrots that will sit on a perch without a chain and not fly away; however, more often than not their wings have been clipped.

Bird room

Any spare space in a house—the loft, a store room or a veranda—can be turned into a bird room. Natural light is vital; the space must get a reasonable amount of sunlight. Any windows should be covered with a mesh screen so that you can open them without risking the loss of your birds. The walls should be painted white to increase the amount of reflected light, where possible with a washable paint to make cleaning easier. For the same reason, the floor should not have joints or gaps between the boards. It is easier to sweep out the dirty sand before spreading clean. Decide on what species of bird you are going to buy before fitting twigs, branches or climbing trees, as they must vary according to the size of the birds. Species which chew everything in sight will attack your window sills, or any exposed wood, so this will have to be protected (with concrete, wire mesh or plastic shields). Nest boxes should be provided for breeding or sleeping in, and you must also fit a suitable bath.

A bird room can make an extremely interesting and attractive parrot house that can provide accommodation for a wide variety of compatible types when chosen carefully.

Loft

The main problem with lofts is the lack of light. Nowadays, though, there are some good attic windows on the market which are very easy to fit yourself and which take care of the ventilation problem, too. Many a parrot lover is thus able to keep whatever species he chooses—mostly Parrakeets—quite happily in his loft and many people breed them very successfully. They are protected from wind and weather, as well as from cats, owls and other nocturnal predators. They can live in perfect peace. The loft can be insulated to suit the sensitivity to cold of whatever breed you have chosen. Here, too, you must take into account the wood chewing habits of your birds!

Balcony

Parrots can also be kept on a suitable balcony. A south-facing one is best but east and west-facing can be just as useful. The first thing to deal with is the question of draughts. These can be eliminated with glass or plastic panels, and to provide a rainproof corner, part of the area should be roofed in. The door to the cage should be such that the birds cannot escape as you go in. The best arrangement is to have double doors with a small space between them, known as a safety porch. With this arrangement, you can enter the aviary and close one door behind you before opening the second door.

A small hatch should lead into the shelter, which the birds enter at night or in bad weather. You can lure them into it in the evening by switching a light on in there.

Garden flight and shelter

An aviary or flight is the ideal for many parrot species, provided that an inner shelter or some protected corner is always accessible. It is a good idea to build this higher than the flight because birds always prefer to roost in the highest possible spot. There are many species which require either gentle heat or even room temperature during the cold season, whereas others are perfectly comfortable in quite severe cold, as long as they have a shelter. An ideal solution would be to have access to your house via a hatch or window.

Most parrot-keepers build an aviary with an attached flight, such as the one on p. 17. The sort you build will depend on the species of bird you choose and your pocket, since many different building materials can be used—stone, wood, concrete, and so on. The more care you take, the better, especially over making it vermin-proof. You should think, first and foremost, of mice, which easily gain access. Of course, it is possible to build in wood and then clad the inside with concrete, particularly if you can fill the space between the two substances with fibreglass or polystyrene as an added buffer against intruders. Windows should always be the largest you can possibly afford, because there can never be too much light reaching the inner spaces, particularly in winter. Double glazing, removable thermopanes, plastic glazing or glass bricks are all good for illumination and protection. The exit hatch is always in the top third, not too large. The windows can be removed completely in the summer to prevent overheating. Certainly, there must be through-ventilation of one sort or another if the glass front faces south.

The best floor surface is a thick layer of cement to keep out vermin.

Next, the flight must be given a cement base; I recommend about 20 cm (8 in) above ground level, and 50 cm (1 ft 8 in) below. This depth keeps out predators as they cannot dig through it. You could use concrete blocks or paving slabs. Build the outer aviary of wood or iron. The former is lighter to

Top: Aviary with access to the house.

Above: Breeding aviary for Australian Parrakeets.

handle and cheaper to buy, but the latter is more durable, though more expensive. It also has the advantage that not a parrot yet has ever chewed its way out of iron! Zinc-coated drainage pipes 4 cm (1½ in) are suitable. The corners are secured with bolts.

A wooden aviary is often constructed out of laths which then have to be

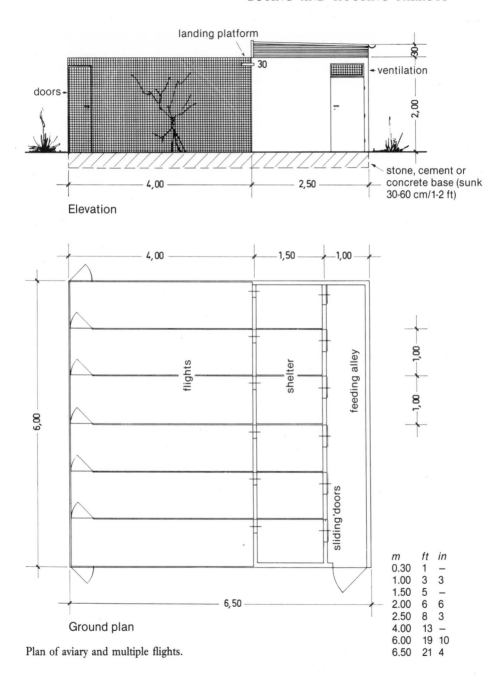

landing platform

30

← ventilation

doors →

stone, cement or
concrete base (sunk
30-60 cm/1-2 ft)

4,00

2,50

2,00

30

Elevation

4,00

1,50

1,00

6,00

1,00

1,00

flights

shelter

feeding alley

sliding doors

6,50

Ground plan

Plan of aviary and multiple flights.

m	ft	in
0.30	1	–
1.00	3	3
1.50	5	–
2.00	6	6
2.50	8	3
4.00	13	–
6.00	19	10
6.50	21	4

weatherproofed (with creosote or wood preservative). When this is dry, zinc-coated mesh is then stapled on. There are various sizes available. Only 9.5 mm ($\frac{3}{8}$ in) wire mesh and 12.5 mm ($\frac{1}{2}$ in) diameter square netting are mouse and weasel proof. If you have several linked cages the dividing mesh can be wider. The standard length of a roll is 25 m (27 yd), the standard widths are 50 and 100 cm (1 ft 8 in and 3 ft 4 in).

The durability of wire netting depends primarily on the thickness of the wire; the average is 0.7 mm ($\frac{1}{32}$ in). You can also get spot-welded square mesh netting which is lighter to work with and more durable, but also costlier. The standard widths of this are 60, 80 and 100 cm (24, 32 and 40 in). The netting needs a coating of some sort for protection (bitumen is best), which you can get from a hardware shop quite cheaply. This has the advantages of drying quickly and not peeling off as easily as lacquer does. Do not coat your netting until several months after erection as it must first remain exposed to the air to oxydize. The coating will then adhere really well. Paint rollers, available in a variety of widths and materials, make the job much easier. Clean them afterwards with petroleum spirit. If you treat your netting in this way every two years, or more frequently, it will last much longer.

Flights which are often attacked by cats can be surrounded with an electric fence, of the sort normally used for keeping animals in a field. The minor shocks deter the cats and the fence only uses minimal electricity.

In winter, it is advisable to have some lighting in the interior to compensate for the shortness of the daylight hours. A practical solution is to install a time switch, either electric or clockwork, so that the lights are switched on automatically at, say, 4 am. The birds then wake up earlier.

It is not practical to plant the inner space with shrubs or flowers because they will be eaten by the birds sooner or later. However, it is important that the birds have a plentiful supply of fresh branches, with bark, so that they can strip it and chew it to their hearts' content, thus obtaining vital nutrients.

You can, however, plant out round the aviary to soften the otherwise hard outlines, but beware of overdoing it. If the birds inside can barely see human beings because of the growth surrounding them, they soon become shy and withdrawn. It has been observed that birds are more sociable towards people in summer than in winter simply because people spend more time outdoors in summer. Roses are very good for planting as screening. On the corners you could put shrub roses, pampas grass or bamboos. Clematis is also suitable, especially if interspersed with annuals, such as begonias, lobelias, tagetes or salvias.

A natural earth floor in the flights can happily be left as it is. Foodstuffs easily become trodden in, and the seeds rapidly germinate, thus providing a good supply of really fresh nourishment, especially important at breeding time. Each month, you can dig it over and watch the rush as the birds fly down and search for seeds, all of which contain many essential minerals.

Feeding, care and breeding

Feeding

Correct feeding is of prime importance to the welfare of pets. In the wild, birds instinctively search out the food that is vital to their well-being: protein, carbohydrate, fats, minerals, and so on. The need for these nutrients varies according to the time of year, or the number of offspring.

This is one reason why it is often difficult for the breeder to gauge the needs accurately, and it is always wise to offer as wide a variety as possible every day. To do this, you need some idea of the constituents of all the foods suitable for parrots.

Canary seed, millet, wheat and maize are all good bulky seeds to feed and they are low in fat content (about 5 per cent) but contain up to 70 per cent carbohydrate and 16 per cent protein. Rich foods, higher in fat content, are sunflower seeds, hemp (but not in its unripe, green stage, as then it is harmful), linseed and niger seed. These all contain some 32 per cent fats, no more than 20 per cent carbohydrate and likewise up to 20 per cent protein.

Larger parrots (Amazons, Cockatoos, African Greys, *Poicephalus*, Macaws, and so on) require a basic diet of about 60–70 per cent sunflower seed combined with wheat, oats, nuts and fruit. For Parrakeets, the percentage of sunflower seed is reduced to 50 or 60, and to this you add canary seed, millet, linseed, wheat, fruit and niger. There are no precise proportions I can give you; sometimes, the bird will want sunflower seed and another day he will prefer canary seed or some other food. It all depends on the time of year, moulting, breeding and so on. The important thing is to offer a variety.

It is best to offer sunflower seeds in a separate container, whereas other seeds can be mixed together. As you clear up the husks, you will soon tell which is the favourite of the day. You should not offer the bird only his favourites. He will always choose his favourite first in any case, which is why I do not like automatic feeders—the birds empty it out to get at the tastiest morsels and the floor is strewn with all the good things they have scorned. If you feed them yourself every day, you can easily balance the diet. If they are hungry, they are more likely to go for the less favoured food. Do not give up when trying out some new items of diet; it is often weeks before the birds will accept it. Naturally, you will observe the bird's reactions—if he sits there, ruffled and withdrawn, be warned. There are birds which would rather starve than try something new. Every bird fancier must develop a feeling for how far he can go before risking harm to his bird.

On no account should parrots be given unnatural food, especially raw meat, which is dangerous and can cause feather plucking.

Some foods can be stored in the deep freeze so that you can offer a wider variety of food in winter than you would otherwise be able to. Hips, hawthorn berries, rowan berries, corn cobs and medlar can be frozen and stored in plastic bags. The evening before you need them, remove them from the freezer. Never give your bird frozen food as this will lead to bowel upsets.

Greenfoods

These are very important because they contain iodine, manganese, common salt and, above all, vitamins.

The commonest source of greenfood is undoubtedly chickweed (*Stellaria media*), not to be confused with the sun spurge (*Euphorbia helioscopia*) which is commonly found in gardens and which is recognized by the milky sap oozing from the broken stems. Chickweed is a very common weed found in gardens, on compost heaps, in fields and graveyards, and in many other places. You can never feed too much fresh chickweed; it must be untainted by chemical sprays. Chickweed is especially valuable for birds which are rearing young. Your birds will not only enjoy the leaves; they are even fonder of the small seed pods, particularly when they are still only at the white, partially ripe stage. Chickweed is available almost the whole year round, provided there is no very severe frost or heavy snowfall. Any weeds which resemble chickweed but have hairy leaves or blue flowers must not be offered as food. Genuine chickweed has smooth leaves and small white flowers.

The leaves as well as the ripe fruits of the dandelion (*Taraxacum officinale*) are always enjoyed. It contains, amongst other things, vitamins, trace elements and calcium. Mangold, spinach and lettuce are also excellent greenfoods. However, be careful with bought lettuce because it may have been sprayed. For this reason, it is probably wiser to grow your own. Too much lettuce, however, especially when it is not absolutely fresh, can lead to bowel upsets or other undesirable consequences. Dwarf lettuces are a good idea, particularly when you have a large number of birds to cater for.

Spiderwort (*Tradescantia*) is also useful. It grows extremely rapidly, which makes it ideal for smaller establishments' needs, but only use tradescantia that has green leaves.

Sprouted seeds

As already mentioned, freshly sprouted seeds are excellent supplements, particularly at breeding time.

For home cultivation, the simplest thing is to make one or more wooden trays on short legs and line them with artificial gauze. Spread this with a layer of wheat, sunflower or other seed and put the trays in the cellar or garden. Sprinkle them with water at least every morning and evening—they must always be damp and never cold. In a few days they will sprout and can be fed to your birds. Do not leave them too long or the birds will refuse them. If you have a large establishment you can make a stack of trays, one on top of the other. The main thing is to keep the air circulating round all of them. Storing your trays in the garden has the disadvantage that wild birds and often mice will attack them, so you must devise a way of protecting them.

Another good natural source of greenfood is found in weed seeds, best fed while they are only partially ripe. I will only mention the commonest and most widespread.

Seedpods of chickweed and the ripe fruits of the dandelion have already been mentioned above. Almost all Parrakeets and especially the Grass Parrakeets love them. The same is true of shepherd's purse (*Capsella bursa-pastoris*), spotted persicaria (*Polygonum persicaria*), cornflower (*Centaurea cyanus*), orache (*Atriplex*), plantain (*Plantago*), chicory (*Cichorium intybus*), marigold (*Calendula*) and all grass seeds. Forget-me-not (*Myosotis*) and pansy (*Viola tricolor*) can also be fed.

Fruit, berries and carrots

Parrots need the vitamins contained in fruit, berries and carrots, as well as those in greenfood. Apples are best of course because they are always available. Among wild berries, particular mention must be made of the fruits of the wild rose, the so-called rose hips. Most species of parrot will eat these and you can find them almost the whole year round as there are species which withstand frost very well. Many parrots also enjoy rowan berries and hawthorn berries, which ripen towards the end of August. For feeding, they must be fully ripe, and can also be dried and stored in this state as well. It is only the seeds of these plants which are eaten. Dried fruit can always be soaked to moisten it. I have never had any luck with elderberries. My birds never took to them, despite repeated attempts. Nevertheless, some species relish them, especially the larger parrots.

Carrots (*roots*) contain carotin (provitamin A), which is a preliminary stage of vitamin A. This is an important factor in fertility. Almost every parrot species will eat carrots enthusiastically, especially when they are fresh and juicy. If they are not, leave them in water for a day.

Additional food for breeding

In the wild almost all birds ingest protein to some extent, and it can be animal protein. An additional food to promote breeding is hard-boiled egg chopped up with crumbled rusk. 100 g (3½ oz) of egg contains 14 g (½ oz) protein, 11 g

21

($\frac{2}{5}$oz) fat, 0.6 g (9 grains) carbohydrate, 74 g (2$\frac{1}{2}$oz) water plus salts, as well as 1.19 mg (8 grains) vitamin A, vitamin D, iron, and so on. A level teaspoonful per bird is normally enough but the amount can be increased when breeding.

There are birds which will not take this mixture, in which case you have to try a proprietary mixture aimed at fussy eaters. It contains dried insects and ant chrysalises and must be moistened with water to a pulp. Some, however, have added fat and so do not need moistening.

Wholemeal bread is often used for rearing young. White bread or rolls must be stale before they are used. Soak them and wring them out before crumbling them up; on no account offer soggy or mushy bread.

Additional feeding of greenfoods, fruit, berries, carrots, eggs, sprouted grain and seeds keeps the birds and their plumage healthy. Rearing will be easier and the offspring large and strong.

Trace elements, minerals, vitamins

Chewing wood is not always mere playfulness or a sign of boredom, but rather, an indicator of a vitamin or hormone deficiency. Apart from cellulose, wood also contains important body-building substances like iron, copper, magnesium, phosphorus, soda, iodine, silicon, as well as other organic elements like saponin, tannin, pectin, sugar, salicylic acid and vitamins. Branches of fruit trees, willows and oaks are best. Sometimes poor feather condition is a result of one of these deficiencies and is improved when such twigs are provided.

Minerals are present in the correct type of sand for birds and in the soil of the aviary floor. However, not every sand is right for birds. Fine white sand is hardly any use because it is mostly quartz. The birds find what they need in calcium fluoride, which also has the advantage of being dust-free. If your garden soil is pure lime, clay or marshy soil, you must spread a thick layer of sand over it.

A supplement of eggshells (crushed), cuttlefish bone or grit helps avoid mineral deficiencies. Some firms sell a composite mineral stone which contains calcium and crushed mussels, amongst other minerals, in a solid block. Raw eggshells have the additional advantage that birds also eat the egg-white which adheres to them, but here you must be sure of feeding only eggs from healthy hens, otherwise you might transfer disease.

Parrots fed in this way should only need vitamin supplements in the winter, and then only small ones. An overdose is not advantageous and can rapidly lead to moulting, which then upsets the whole moulting cycle. Often, people avoid feeding multivitamins because vitamin B1 gives off a strong smell, so it is only given once a week on a titbit. It is difficult to state an exact dosage because this varies with the size of the bird. A healthy budgerigar can take one or two drops a week, a larger parrot slightly more.

Since some vitamin preparations are not soluble in water, it is better to look for a soluble type, which is readily taken in water by all species. 20 ml of one of these solutions contains:

500,000 IE vitamin A
100,000 IE vitamin D3
20 mg vitamin E acetate
25 mcg vitamin B1
34.2 mcg riboflavin-5'-sodium phosphate
50 mcg vitamin K3 sodium bisulphate
20 mcg folic acid

The soluble vitamins only come in small amounts because, once opened, they must be used up quickly. Many of them evaporate and become unusable if exposed to air for any length of time.

Hints on care

If you want healthy parrots, there are certain basic rules that you must observe.

Large parrots in particular are adversely affected by poor oxygen content in the air. They hang their heads, screw their eyes up and even breathe through open beaks. The higher the temperature, the lower is the oxygen content. Therefore, always aim for a well-ventilated but draught-free area at normal temperature. Only newly-imported birds need a warmed room, and that just in the early days.

A parrot kept in a room of your house should have a shower in lukewarm water at least once a week in order to get rid of the feather dust. A plant spray is ideal for the purpose. Birds with plumage problems, or which have moulted unevenly, can be sprayed with a mixture of water and rum or brandy—but do not spray the head! A trace of alcohol encourages feather growth and improves the appearance of the plumage. Large parrots are best sprayed on their stands or in the garden, when they are tame enough. If they are not that tame, remove the tray and feeders and put the cage in the bath before spraying the bird *in situ*.

Be careful when cutting claws.

Avoid soiled feet because dried-on droppings can lead to inflammation. The first rule of bird care is, therefore, to keep the cage clean. Only trim the claws when the bird really is in danger of getting stuck on the bars and hanging helplessly there, which often happens when the claws become more curved than normal, like a sickle. Bird-shop owners will come to your aid here, as, of course, will vets. If you are experienced and skilled enough, you can do it yourself. Always cut at an angle, as shown on page 23. Never cut too much because each claw has a blood vessel, which can often be seen against the light in pale claws.

Some general tips on breeding

Breeders always designate the sexes of their breeding birds by two figures separated by a comma; the figure before the comma is the number of males and that after the comma, the females. For example: 3,6 = 3 males and 6 females; 0,3 = 3 females; and 1,1 = 1 male and 1 female.

Sexing many parrot species is very difficult and a breeder may have to be patient for a long time until he can be sure of the sex of his birds. Often, it is a matter of experience, and you can only rely on what the vendor tells you and trust him to be honest with you, or conclude the deal with a guarantee of sex. However, even an experienced dealer cannot be certain of the sex of birds of many species. It is the exception that proves the rule. For example, I once had a female Splendid Parrakeet which had red feathers on the wing band, and a beautifully marked male Golden-mantled Rosella which had the small head typical of a female. Such 'mistakes' of nature are, however, rare and isolated incidents. Maturity varies greatly among the parrot species. With the smaller types, maturity is often reached by the early age of six months, but many of the larger species are not ready for breeding until they are four to six years old. Full colouring of the plumage is no indication. The opposite, however, does hold true—lack of full colouring usually means that the bird cannot yet be ready for breeding; such as the Crimson Rosella that is still green.

It is always advantageous to mate a female with an older male, but whenever two birds are mated for the first time, you must keep a careful eye on them. A male can pursue his female to the point of exhaustion. In such a case, it would be advisable to clip the male's wings a little to curtail his flying.

In the wild, the desire to breed is dependent on light and temperature, thus ensuring a natural period of rest for the birds. This is often not the case in heated bird rooms or aviaries. The pairs find themselves in constant breeding conditions under the artificial lighting, so they breed on and on until they eventually weaken and even die. The offspring, too, become poorer and lack the vitality of 'normal' young. The best way to overcome this is to reduce the temperature in plenty of time and remove the breeding chambers from use by blocking them up. Or you can separate the sexes. In addition, avoid all special food supplements; for example, give no hemp, little germinated seed and only very little animal protein (hard-boiled egg, and so on).

It is always wise to cease breeding from October until March, except, of course, for those species which normally only breed in the winter (for example, Brown's Rosella).

An overweight bird will show little interest in breeding. Some species are more inclined to obesity than others, and this will be less of a problem in large flights than with caged birds. It is wise not to feed these birds too much oily seed.

If you have several aviaries joined together, you must take care to put compatible species side by side. If birds of the same species or genus are placed side by side, the resultant friction can hinder breeding. Therefore, for example, do not put different Rosellas in neighbouring pens; instead, separate them by another species (Golden-mantled Rosella, then Cockatiel, Blue or Mealy Rosella, then Redrump Parrakeet, followed by Stanley Rosella, and Bourke's Parrakeet, and so on). The mating drive of a male Golden-mantled Rosella cannot be directed at a female Blue or Mealy Rosella if there is a flight full of Cockatiels between them. You do not need double netting between flights when you house the species in this way because no quarrels arise.

Birds will only breed if they feel completely safe and secure.

Nest sites

Parrots nest in holes. Of all the types mentioned in this book, only the Quaker Parrakeet does not, but even this nests in holes when in captivity. Some species prefer shallow holes and others deep ones, and this varies within species, too, so always offer them a choice of breeding holes. They will soon make their choice, and from then on leave that nest in precisely the same spot and remove the unwanted sites. The size of a breeding hole will vary with the size of the bird, as must the size of the entrance hole. Never make the nest hole too big. Larger and more ungainly species like a perch to land on in front of the entrance. It is of the utmost importance that you should be able to open the nest, in order to keep a weather eye on the eggs and young.

It is possible to provide ready-made nest holes cut out of tree trunks of various sizes. Since they most closely resemble the natural sites, they are often preferred by many parrot species. They have the added advantage of thickness, which makes them proof against wood-chewing species, particularly when they are of oak or beech. The interior temperature of these breeding logs is even, and their thickness gives added protection against outside noise, so the more sensitive birds feel secure in them.

25

Left: Crimson Rosella in front of a natural log nest site.

Right: A view from the rear into the nest of a Masked Lovebird, which builds a domed nest out of strips of bark.

Positioning a deep box on a slope helps to prevent the eggs from being trampled on (especially important when you have Princess Alexandra Parrakeets). It is also easier for the young to emerge from these. If the sides are particularly steep and smooth, you should also fix wire netting, large staples or strips of wood (ladder-like) up the side to help the birds climb out.

Nesting sites must be waterproof and safe from mice. For broods that require a certain amount of moisture, set the log into the earth, so that damp can rise up it, and protect the base against mice by putting a layer of netting across it. In shallow boxes, keep the peat-litter moistened, but do not overdo it. The best nesting material base is a mixture of turf, earth and wood shavings.

Brooding and hatching

Some individuals do not resent being observed whilst brooding, others are very upset by being disturbed, and abandon the eggs. The point about observation is that it enables you to detect and remove infertile eggs after about a week. You can tell an infertile egg because it is quite clear when held up to the light. Fertile eggs, on the other hand, show a few red veins at first, and later become quite dark and opaque. Only the wide upper end remains light. Dead young must be removed with all speed.

If the female has laid but does not sit, her eggs can be put under another broody female, but this often only succeeds when the species are closely related. Parrakeets often take to the Redrump Parrakeet as a foster-mother, either for the eggs or for 'problem' youngsters. Even here, however, there have been disappointments.

Young which have an empty crop should be examined again in the evening. If the crop is still empty, the breeder must take swift action to save the bird. The best implement for this job is a so-called single-shot dropper, obtainable from a chemist. Instead of the glass tube, fit a 3–5 cm ($1\frac{1}{4}$–2 in) length of rubber tubing (cycle valve rubber, for instance) and slide this down the throat into the bird's crop. On no account fill the crop to the limit, it must always retain its soft flexibility. The food can be a mixture of baby cereal, oats and dextrose. Add a vitamin drop every third day.

A youngster without feathers must be fed every two hours during the day. Later on, depending on the size and genus, this can be reduced to every three or four hours.

Clean the nest out thoroughly after every brood, paying particular attention to mites, and provide clean nesting material.

Illness

Compared to other birds, parrots are less susceptible to illness. If a bird appears unwell and you do not know the cause of the illness or the treatment for it, you should take it to a vet immediately. He will want to know the main symptoms. Acute illnesses are more easily detected than insidious ones, since often the only signs of the latter are loss of weight and appetite. The bird perches motionless with ruffled feathers and somewhat drooping wings, and sleeps more often than is usual in the daytime. Glazed and apathetic eyes are a sure sign of advanced ill-health. The vet must be consulted immediately if the bird shows any of the following symptoms: discharge of mucous from the nostrils, together with shaking of the head, inflammation of the eyes and strong continuous trembling. Noisy or irregular breathing, or shortage of breath are also abnormal. Watery or discoloured motions and soiled undertail-coverts must also receive prompt veterinary attention.

Parasitic infection

Worms

A prevalent problem in recent years is the presence of worms. Again and again deaths are reported which can be traced back to severe worm infestation. Often the birds evince no obvious symptoms; they simply sit on their perches looking miserable, only to be found dead in the aviary one morning. As long as a certain balance is maintained between the parasite and the host, no clear symptoms of ill-health are exhibited. However, the situation can be altered dramatically by one minute factor (such as, vitamin deficiency or cold), so that the bird is no longer capable of holding the parasite in check.

We are concerned primarily with specific roundworms (*ascaridia*), hairworms (*capillaria*) and threadworms (*heterakis*). The first can be up to 6 cm (2½ in) in length and inhabit the small intestine. Hairworms also live in the small intestine, but are common in the gizzard and the crop as well. They are very thin and only some 2 cm (¾ in) long. They bore, head first, into the intestinal mucous membrane, which can cause bleeding, as a result of which the bird's excreta take on a brownish tinge.

The eggs are visible in the droppings (not in the white part) at 100 × magnification. However, accurate diagnosis of the type is only possible at 200 or 300× magnification. A small amount of excreta is dropped into a saturated solution of salt and some fifteen minutes later a drop from the surface is placed on a glass slide, covered with a glass plate and viewed through the microscope. Roundworms have an elongated form, are double walled and have zigzag markings on the interior. Hairworms are only about half their size but longer and show, at each end, a so-called embolus (bulge). Their eggs have a double casing. You do sometimes see atypical circular eggs which have black centres. There are also traces of starch, plant remains and sometimes food mites, but these are harmless if they are not prevalent.

You do not necessarily find eggs in every dropping (which should always be analyzed while fresh), but on the other hand, very badly infested birds have been known to have a horrific number of eggs in one sample. Eggs only develop in humid weather and are very resilient. An egg taken in by a bird hatches out in the intestine and grows into a mature worm. Roundworms take about two months, but hairworms only about three weeks, to develop.

Treatment Roundworms can be eradicated by using a piperazine product, either in solution in the drinking water or by direct administration. The dosage is according to the size of the species—consult your vet. It has to be taken in three repeated dosages at intervals of three weeks in dry weather conditions. If you are giving the dosage in solution, keep the bird off liquids for the previous half day. However, there are now better preparations.

Prof. Frank has done trials with Thenbendazole (Panacur) (from Hoechst) and they have shown no side effects. The product comes as a suspension— 2.5 per cent, 1 litre or 10 per cent, 2.5 ml (= $\frac{1}{4}$ litre). There is also Panacur powder (veterinary) at 4 per cent, 500 g. For this, you calculate on 30–50 mg per kg of bodyweight. Smaller birds, or those that do not drink much, are given more. The surest method is to put it directly into the crop whenever possible. The powder dissolves well in water to give a milky-looking fluid. Levamisole (ICI) can also be recommended.

Since several species drink far too little and since, above all, the persistent threadworm is much more difficult to combat, you can inject the fluid directly. Slip 3–4 cm ($1\frac{1}{4}$–$1\frac{1}{2}$ in) (depending on the size of the bird) of cycle valve rubber on to a dropper and fill it with 1 cu cm of dilute Levamisole. Introduce the valve rubber into the crop, though this is almost impossible with some species (such as the King Parrakeet). After only a few hours the worms recede. A friend of mine had a Splendid Parrakeet with twenty-seven worms! However, before undertaking such treatment, you must always make sure that your bird really is heavily infested. All medications are potentially harmful. It is also possible to have such a knotted mass of worms that they cannot be ejected. In such a case the worms do in fact die but they remain inside the bird, giving rise to such a toxic slough that the bird will still succumb. You must give a further course of treatment after about three weeks to annihilate those worms which have developed in the interim.

Naturally, the floor of the aviary will be strewn with eggs during a severe infestation and it will not be easy to get rid of them. The surest way is to burn them off with a flamethrower (use a blowlamp in a small aviary). A more difficult and costly way is to remove the topsoil and renew it. There are also liquids which destroy parasite eggs, coccidia, bacteria, viruses and mites. Every aviary floor should be dug over thoroughly and frequently. Check for worm infestation every year, especially if you want to introduce new birds to your collection.

Mites and feather mites

There are a variety of these, the most well-known of which is the red mite (*Dermanyssus avium*). These creatures only feed on their host at night, disappearing by day into every surrounding nook and cranny. In a severe infestation the birds become very anaemic and young birds in particular can easily succumb. Cages, perches and nest boxes must all be treated several times with insecticide because one application will not destroy all the existing eggs. You must also dust the bird with insecticide powder (such as Glutox).

Recently, the mange mite (*Cnemidocoptes*) has become more widespread. One form attacks the feet and causes so-called leg calcification. The chalky nodules are easily removed by repeated rubbing with olive oil. Another excellent medium is Mesulphen BPC.

Another troublesome mange mite attacks the beak and also affects the legs and area around the vent. A greyish coating spreads over the base of the beak and beneath the eyes but, if noticed early enough, can quickly be removed with olive oil or Mesulphen again. If you ignore this mite it can cause beak deformity. The young are often infected whilst being fed by their parents. It is particularly common among Budgerigars, but birds of the genus *Cyanoramphus* are also particularly vulnerable.

A variety of insecticides can be used against feather mites and quill mites (*Mallophaga*), which are constantly present on birds. They feed on the feathers and head scales. In severe infestations you can see the nits (eggs) on the shafts of the small feathers. A dichlorvos strip is also effective against mites. You hang a strip in the room and it goes on working for about four months. Neither the bird nor its food should come into contact with the strip.

Fungus infections

Fungus infections are extremely dangerous. They have lately become far more frequent and often are not recognized as such. Many people attribute the increase to the indiscriminate use of antibiotics, and also to increased susceptibility as a result of parasite attacks and other debilitating illnesses.

Aspergillosis

Aspergillus fumagatus is one member of this group. The spores are breathed into the bronchial tubes or enter on mouldy foodstuffs. It has been found on millet. Unfortunately it cannot be detected with the naked eye. Affected birds often breath through open beaks, but some have been known to die without showing any visible signs. Greenish fungi are found on the bronchial organs and are the probable cause of death. If called in early enough, a vet can be of help.

Thrush

Candida albicans is another fungus that can often be found on foodstuffs. It mainly settles in the crop, oesophagus, pharynx and on the beak. Affected parts become swollen and lined with a grey substance. In this case, too, the vet can only help if called in as soon as the infection becomes apparent.

Other ailments

Feather plucking

Occasionally some species, especially the larger psittacines, take to plucking their own feathers. This is a great problem, the causes of which are varied. Most probably the following factors are involved: dietary deficiency; wrong feeding; boredom; dry air; an unfulfilled desire to mate; and other psychological problems.

Some birds pluck themselves bald, others bite their feathers off. Unfortunately, there is seldom anything to be done about it. Correct feeding may help—plenty of vitamins, minerals and high protein foodstuffs, fresh twigs, carrots, apples, and so on—all of which could also occupy the bird's attention. It is particularly important to 'fuss over your birds' with the larger species. Raw meat, chocolate or spicy human foods could cause skin irritations that eventually lead to the bird becoming a feather plucker. Sometimes a change of environment helps—another cage, an aviary in a different location. Success is sometimes achieved if you paint on a bitter substance (tincture of aloes). Either way, as soon as you see signs that feather plucking is beginning, employ one of these remedies immediately.

Egg binding

This is fairly unusual in psittacines, unless they are being asked to breed too intensively. A humid atmosphere, a smear of oil and gentle massaging of the abdomen in the direction of the cloaca can do much to help move the egg.

The sooner you detect egg binding, the quicker and easier it is to do something about it. The female will usually leave the nest and may stay on the floor of the cage or on her perch with her rump feathers stiffly erect and her eyes shut. It sometimes happens that she stays in the nest box and you know nothing about her problem because you are trying not to disturb her.

Overgrown beaks and toenails

Unfortunately this does happen sometimes. Thicker, rougher perches will ensure more wear on claws, as will calcium or grit for the beak. The problem could be caused by lack of vitamins A and D.

Inflammation of the eyes

You must take the bird to the vet, especially if it is newly imported, because an eye inflammation is usually a result of infection, not of an injury. Sometimes a cold in the bronchial system is the cause. Infected birds must be isolated and treated with a broad spectrum antibiotic. Pay particular attention to this problem in imported Amazons.

Virus infections

Ornithosis/psittacosis

This is the most notorious disease, which, years ago, usually proved fatal. Nowadays, it has been controlled by means of quarantine and the antibiotics tetracyclin and chloramphenicol. The irritants are found in the stool and the blood. There appears to be a variety of pathogens, each posing a different degree of danger. The disease can be passed on to humans via the faeces or particles. There are no symptoms typical solely of this disease.

Newcastle's disease

This is an atypical fowlpest which parrots can contract. It is fatal; there is no known cure. Threatened birds can be immunized with live vaccine. It is not transmittable to humans and is rare in parrots. Signs of this illness are: loss of appetite, breathing difficulties, diarrhoea, hanging the head, congestion, loss of balance and a completely apathetic posture.

Bacterial infections

Recently, the salmonella strain *Salmonella typhimurium* has been on the increase. This is mostly found in African Greys and Amazons, primarily amongst newly imported birds.

Tame, talking housepets

Irrespective of breed, no parrot will imitate words or sounds until it is reasonably tame. Therefore, the owner's first priority must be to get his bird used to him and gradually tame it. This can only be achieved with great calm, persistence and evenness of temperament on the part of the enthusiast. Parrots in particular have extremely good memories and one error can ruin them for life.

The younger the bird, the easier it is to tame. Birds which are not caught until they are older seldom become tame. In some species, you can tell a youngster by the incompleteness of the plumage colouring; the iris, feet and beak colouration can also be good indicators. Of course, you need to know what the mature bird should look like (in my descriptions of the various genera I give characteristic markings of the adults and often of the immature birds, too).

One bird kept by itself in a room will become tame more quickly than two or more in the same room, even if they are caged separately. A parrot should regard human beings as companions. Most parrots are quieter alone; put several together and they soon begin trying to outdo each other in volume.

Some species are naturally good talkers (such as the African Grey) and others are more talented at movement, both imitative and playful (Cockatoos, Amazons). It is not often that both talents are found in the same bird. Like people, their characteristics and inclinations vary from one to another and the character of the owner is not that of his bird. All you can say is that, as a rule, an African Grey is an extremely talented imitator but not always a particularly affectionate or friendly companion. He rarely loses his natural mistrust completely.

Cockatoos, on the other hand, do little verbal imitating as a rule (crested ones even less than the others). They are very good-natured and tend to go in for copying acrobatics or specific actions. Amazons are noisy and usually well-behaved but vary widely in imitative talents and make noises which are (compared with the talented talkers) always somewhat parrot-like.

Taming

It is best to transfer your new arrival straight to the cage that you intend for his home, for two reasons: firstly, you do not know if he bites, and secondly, it avoids the risk of him becoming hand-shy. Until you know each other better, leave the cage in the same spot—a quite corner out of draughts or full midday sun, but not dark. For the first few weeks, leave the parrot alone to get thoroughly used to people and to his new surroundings. Put his food in slowly and cautiously as you speak calmly to him. Some birds begin to trust you quite quickly and others need a little more time. Hold a tempting titbit of carrot or apple or millet to the bars of his cage and wait patiently. If he does not approach, wedge the morsel between the bars and try again next day.

Once he will happily eat from your hand, it is time to progress. After a little while, open the cage door and repeat the whole process through there, just as cautiously and patiently as before. Gradually build up to the point when the bird will let you caress him through the bars and later through the open door. One day, try slipping your hand or just one finger under his feet so that he is sitting on your hand, though still in his cage. When this has succeeded several times, you will be able to bring him out of the cage on your hand— just as cautiously and steadily as before—and put him back straight away. After yet more time has gone by, lift him out on to his cage roof or a stand. Later on, he will come and go at will.

Some parrots arrive with one wing already clipped, usually carried out by someone in their country of origin. After moulting the feathers will grow and then it is up to the owner to decide whether to clip them again (for large parrots, 4–7cm ($1\frac{1}{2}$–$2\frac{3}{4}$ in) is enough).

Many parrots show strong individual preferences where people are concerned. Some prefer children, others the lady or man of the house. Quite often, male birds prefer ladies, and vice versa, but it is not always so. Nor is it necessarily the 'hand that feeds' which is favoured.

Imitation

Only relaxed birds talk, and the trainer must speak slowly and clearly. Ladies' or children's voices are clearer and therefore imitated more successfully than men's. Parrots find it relatively easy to copy the vowels *a e o u*, so at first it is a good idea to teach words where these sounds are dominant, such as nanna, mamma, coco. Do your best to avoid sibilants, however, and always keep practising the old words even when you are teaching new ones.

Use the same words for an event every time: 'Goodbye' when you go out; 'Hello, Coco' when you come in; 'Good morning' early in the day; and so on. Some parrots are imitative geniuses and others are less gifted. Some learn tunes better, or coughing, clicking the tongue, laughing, sneezing or other noises. Some African Greys have become famous for imitating practically every sound in their environment—up to a hundred phrases or sayings, whole songs, some even in different languages. The imitation can even be so good that it is impossible to distinguish the parrot voice from the human one.

The more human sounds a bird can copy, the less he uses his natural voice.

Modern technology makes it possible for you to record set phrases on a continuous loop tape and play that back to your bird, if you so wish. In this way, a talented bird could pick up several things to imitate.

Often even the quietest bird takes it into his head that he must outdo the volume of radio, vacuum cleaner, television or any other 'noise boxes' you may have. A screeching bird is best treated in the following manner: cover his cage with a thick black cloth for a while so that he is left in total darkness. If you are strict about this for several days it will get through to the bird and he will soon give up.

Psittacines are often able to connect certain sounds with certain actions. If you sway to music, your parrot will soon copy you and think that music and movement must go together.

With some species, (Budgies, Cockatiels) it is the males who are more easily tamed, and who also have a better capacity for imitation. However, this does not appear to be so among larger species (African Greys, Amazons, etc.).

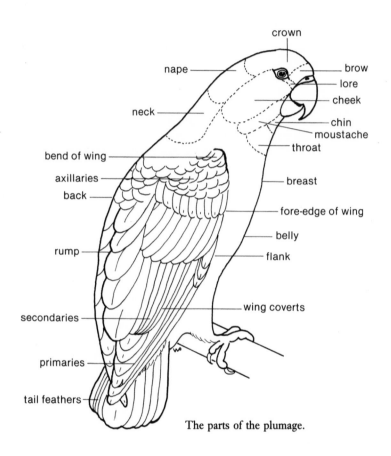

crown

nape

brow

lore

cheek

chin

moustache

throat

neck

bend of wing

axillaries

back

breast

fore-edge of wing

belly

rump

flank

secondaries

wing coverts

primaries

tail feathers

The parts of the plumage.

Parrot genera

Black- and White-beaked Cockatoos (*Kakatoe*)

Black-beaked Cockatoos

Umbrella Cockatoo *K. alba*
Salmon-crested Cockatoo *K. moluccensis*
Greater Sulphur-crested Cockatoo *K. galeritus* (8 races)
Lesser Sulphur-crested Cockatoo *K. sulphurea* (6 races)

White-beaked Cockatoos

Rose-breasted Cockatoo *K. roseicapilla* (2 races)
Red-vented Cockatoo *K. haematuropygia*
Leadbeater's Cockatoo *K. leadbeateri*

Origin and habit: Philippines to Australia. Cockatoos are among the largest parrots of the ancient world. Without exception they all have a crest of one type or another. They are good fliers and climbers but very poor at walking. They live in large colonies, searching for food in close liaison.

Their food is fruits, berries, grain and all kinds of seeds, as well as roots and bulbs. They breed in holes in trees, hollow branches and some even in crevices in rocks. The usual clutch is two to five eggs. The natives frequently take the young from the nests and hand-rear them, thus they are very tame.
General remarks: Like Macaws, many Cockatoos arrive in Europe half-tamed, especially the Lesser Sulphur-crested Cockatoo, closely followed by the Greater Sulphur-crested Cockatoo. The White-beaked Cockatoos are not as common on the market. All Cockatoos are very social and seek company.

This makes them only too happy to attach themselves to humans. They make a favourite of anyone who will keep them company, caress them and pay attention to them. No other parrot is as affectionate as the Cockatoo.

They are willing to pick up all sorts of tricks and can be uniquely amusing. However, they are not such good talkers as African Greys and Amazons. Some never lose their natural voice and others are quiet and unobtrusive.

The name is said to come from Malay (Kaka = father, tua = old). They live to a great age—one was even kept for over 100 years.

Food: Sunflower seeds, soaked maize, wheat, oats, canary seed, millet, carrots, fruit, nuts, lettuce, dandelions and chickweed. At first, many are fussy eaters.

Housing and rearing. In the house: Cockatoos need a great deal of tender loving care and entertainment, so if you buy one you must treat it as a member of the family and give it plenty of your time. They are not great talkers but they are more amusing companions than any other species. Those that are tame can be let out frequently but, if full winged, they are liable to damage the furniture. Fix a perch or climbing branch to the cage for daytime use. It is best to keep a Cockatoo as your sole bird because, if obtained when young, it may soon learn to trust you and will love to be stroked.

The cage must have an especially well-constructed fastening because a Cockatoo's strong beak can open or destroy all sorts of things. In general, males are tamer than females. The male of a White Cockatoo has black eyes and the female red-brown eyes, except in the case of the Bare-eyed and Slender-billed Cockatoos.

In the garden: Almost all species are hardy and almost impervious to frost. For winter quarters they need a flight with a dry and draught-proof inner shelter, neither of which should be of wood because this would soon be destroyed.

A pair will only remain tame and trusting until they want to breed. Then beware! Their temperament can change totally, and they may attack and bite. Build the nest boxes of stout wood (preferably a hardwood) or use a natural tree trunk. Different species have been known to hybridize, even when of greatly differing sizes.

Cockatoos have also been kept flying free. One pair even bred in a barrel that had been sunk into the earth for water fowl.

Black-beaked Cockatoos

Umbrella Cockatoo (*K. alba*) Molucca and Halmahera (illustrated p. 39)

Characteristics: 40–45 cm (15¾–17¾ in) long. Male—white; bare bluish-white eye patches; iris, feet and beak black. Female—red-brown iris.

The Umbrella Cockatoo is one of the less frequently available of the Cockatoos, although it cannot be described as rare. I once met a very attractive and affectionate specimen, of which I can only speak highly. A successful mating was reported in 1972 and one nestling survived. The aviary was 20 m (65 ft) long and the nest box 50 × 40 × 50 cm (20 × 15¾ × 20 in).

Salmon-crested or Moluccan Cockatoo (*K. moluccensis*) South Moluccas

Characteristics: 50 cm (20 in) long. Male—white with a delicate pink tinge, crest pink, tail feathers cream, iris dark. Female—narrower head, less pink

Left: Study of the head of an Umbrella Cockatoo.

Right: The Lesser Sulphur-crested Cockatoo quickly becomes tame.

tinge, tail feathers yellowish, iris dark brown. Immature—often no pink tinge until one or two years old.

This Cockatoo is no stranger in the dealers' shops, although it is never imported in large numbers. It is never cheap; many imported specimens are already tame. It makes use of its very powerful voice if it feels neglected. It is able to raise both its crest and its moustache feathers, indicating its mood. They have a lovable character, and some are very good talkers and have other imitative talents. Tame Salmon-crests can be left under supervision on a stand or tree in the garden if one wing has been clipped. They have been bred on a number of occasions in Europe and the USA.

Greater Sulphur-crested Cockatoo (*K. galeritus*) Australia, Tasmania, New Guinea and South East Islands

Characteristics: 50 cm (20 in) long. Male—white; crest yellow, area around ears yellowish; iris, feet and beak black. Female—iris red-brown.

39

This species is commonly exported, except the Australian race. Males become more tame than do females. They are very hardy and quick to learn. In the case of one captive pair, at the end of May the female laid two eggs in a decaying willow tree. Both birds worked on the hole to increase the size of the nesting site. The female sat at night and the male mostly took care of the day shift. At first the young had flesh coloured beaks, which became grey-black over the weeks. The first one left the nest at eleven weeks. It was still smaller than its parents. During this time, the birds consumed large quantities of hemp, egg, softened white bread, carrots, radishes and strawberries but their favourite was cooked barley. In 1879 one youngster and in 1880 two were hatched in a cage measuring 80×50 cm ($31\frac{1}{2} \times 20$ in) in Algeria. Greater Sulphur-crested Cockatoos do not need heat in winter.

Lesser Sulphur-crested Cockatoo (*K. sulphurea*) Sulawesi, Lombok, Sumbawa, Flores, Sumba and Timor (illustrated pp. 39 and 41)

Characteristics: 32–36 cm ($12\frac{1}{2}$–14 in) long. Male—white; crest and ears yellow to deep orange (depending on race); iris, beak and feet black. Female—iris red-brown. Young—pale beak and feet. Iris begins to colour definitively around two

Page 41
Top left: Two male Citron-crested Cockatoos (*Kakatoe s. citrinocristata*); this is one of the six races of Lesser Sulphur-crested Cockatoos
Top right: Rose-breasted Cockatoo (*Kakatoe*, also *Eolophus*, *roseicapilla*)
Bottom left: Leadbeater's Cockatoo (*Kakatoe Leadbeateri*)
Bottom right: Red-vented Cockatoo (*Kakatoe haematuropygia*)

Page 42
Top left: Princess of Wales Parrakeet (*Polytelis alexandrae*)
Top right: Crimson-winged Parrakeet (*Aprosmictus erythropterus erythropterus*)
Bottom: Cockatiels, one of natural colouring and one pied

Page 43
Top left: Green-winged King Parrakeet (*Alisterus chloropterus*)
Top right: Australian King Parrakeet (*Alisterus scapularis*)
Bottom left: Amboina King Parrakeet (*Alisterus amboinensis*)
Bottom right: Crimson Rosella (*Platycercus elegans*)

Page 44
Top left: Blue Rosella or Mealy Rosella (*Platycercus adscitus palliceps* (subspecies))
Top right: Adelaide Rosella (*Platycercus adelaide*)
Bottom left: Yellow-fronted Parrakeet or Kakariki (*Cyanoramphus auriceps*)
Bottom right: Manycolour Parrakeet (*Psephotus varius*)

years, complete after three or four years. One race, the Citron-crested Cockatoo, has an orange crest and another orange ear markings.

Lesser Sulphur-crested Cockatoos were formerly the most commonly imported. Their voice is not as powerful as that of the previous species. Breeding has often succeeded. During courtship the male circles round his chosen female, bowing and hopping as he makes enticing calls. He raises his crest and mutual preening begins. Two or three eggs are laid, which take twenty-eight days to hatch. As in all White Cockatoos, the male sits during the day and his partner at night.

The young are fledged at about three months. Each parent feeds one youngster, who beats his wings during the whole process. After some two weeks they begin to feed themselves. As soon as the parents show signs of renewed mating desire, you have to remove the young because their parents may attack them. Lesser Sulphur-crested Cockatoos have been bred successfully in unheated quarters.

For breeding, offer them fresh corn cobs, egg and squeezed-out white bread as supplements.

White-beaked Cockatoos

Rose-breasted or Roseate Cockatoo (*K.* also *Eolophus, roseicapilla*)
Australia (illustrated p. 41)

Characteristics: 38 cm (15 in) long. Male—upper parts grey; head, neck, breast and belly pink; crest small and broad; iris black; broad band of pink above the eye socket. Female—red-brown iris; narrow band of pink above the eye socket. Young—dark iris; underparts pink mixed with grey. Coloration of iris not complete until four or five years of age. Young males identified by the broad band of pink above the eye socket, young females by the narrow one.

This parrot is very common in its homeland. Large flocks swoop down on to the wheat fields, which makes the birds very unpopular with farmers. As a result of this, huge numbers are shot, or removed from the nests to be tamed (but the latter is illegal).

There is a law permitting the shooting of the birds but prohibiting their removal for taming. When I was in Australia in 1975, I heard that new laws were about to be enacted. Many of the hollow nest sites in the trunks of the eucalyptus trees are hacked open and the nestlings are removed, and in some trees you can still find the wire snares which were used to catch the birds by the neck before they were fished out. Their only natural enemy is the Australian Broadtailed Eagle, which feeds its young mostly on these parrots.

Rose-breasted Cockatoos have a very interesting aerial mating display. Their nests are usually built in dead eucalyptus or rubber trees and

45

Typical nesting tree for Rose-breasted Cockatoos. The bark has been removed and the bare patch polished.

upholstered inside with small twigs. One other peculiarity of the Rose-breasted Cockatoo is that it is the only Cockatoo species which lifts its foot *over* its wing to scratch its head, whereas other sorts raise their feet directly to the head.

The following observation has not been fully explained yet: the breeding pair bite off all the bark beneath the entrance hole and then proceed to polish this bald spot every day, until it is quite smooth. On crooked branches they only polish the interior surface. Is this a defence against marauders? The Rose-breasted is the most frequently bred Cockatoo in captivity. They lay from two to six eggs, which take twenty-three or twenty-four days to hatch (according to Dr Kolar, twenty-one days). The parents take it in turns to incubate, though the female sits longest. The male shares the feeding. After about seven weeks the young emerge from the nest and are fed and preened by their parents for a further three or four weeks. Two broods a year are not uncommon.

In captivity, too, these Cockatoos carry small twigs and leaves into the nest, tear them into fragments and construct a nest lining with them. In some cases, the would-be parents removed a lining of peat-litter or sawdust completely before starting to breed. This is probably because they require a certain amount of moisture for breeding sites, as is the case with Lovebirds.

The best food during the rearing period is as follows: first and foremost, plenty of germinated sunflower seeds, with oats and wheat, and seed capsules from chickweed and shepherd's purse. Also offer crumbled up white bread mixed with egg. Cockatoos have a partiality for pecking up seedlings from the aviary floor. Fresh corn on the cob is excellent food but unfortunately is only available towards the end of summer, when the young are already half grown, therefore frozen cobs, well thawed, can be offered at other times.

Size of nestbox: 50×50 cm (20×20 in) and 2 m (60 in) deep, made of stout planks of natural wood, still with the bark on. Successful broods have been obtained from a box measuring 35×35 cm $\times 55$ cm ($13\frac{3}{4} \times 13\frac{3}{4} \times 21\frac{3}{4}$ in) deep. The entrance hole should have a diameter of 9 cm ($3\frac{1}{2}$ in), with a landing board in front of it. Breeders usually make the interior too large. In the wild, it is very small and narrow, often such that the youngsters have to sit on top of each other. Flights should be 3–4 m (9 ft 9 in–13 ft) long and 2 m (6 ft 6 in) high, with an inner shelter of 2×1.5 m (6 ft 6 in $\times$ 5 ft). If these Cockatoos have enough twigs and branches in the flight, they only chew them moderately. They can be unheated in the winter.

They are not naturally talented talkers, but restrict themselves to a few phrases. However, they will quickly pick up a few tricks. Kept alone in a cage, these Cockatoos become very tame and trusting.

Red-vented or Philippine Cockatoo (*K. haematuropygia*) Philippines, Palawan (illustrated p. 41)

Characteristics: 32 cm ($12\frac{1}{2}$ in) long. Male—white; small broad crest; undertail coverts vermilion; iris black-brown. Female—iris red-brown.

Until the late 1970s you seldom found this Cockatoo on sale, and practically nothing had been written about it. It has been bred in the USA. In 1968 I was lucky enough to see more than twenty of these Cockatoos in a dealer's shop in Hamburg. They appeared very gentle and calm, and many were very tame. Their smallness of stature made them very desirable.

Leadbeater's Cockatoo (*K. leadbeateri*) Australia (illustrated p. 41)

Characteristics: 39 cm ($15\frac{1}{4}$ in) long. Male—upper parts white; under parts pink; brow red; transverse stripes on crest of white-red-yellow; iris black. Female—red-brown iris. Young—at around three years old the iris of the female becomes red-brown.

They have become rare in some parts of Australia. They do not live on the coast, preferring the interior, where they spend much time on the ground, looking for grass seed, roots, tubers and the pips of the bitter melon. Now that Australia forbids the export of birds, Leadbeaters are rare in captivity.

It is the most beautiful of all Cockatoos, a jewel in any collection. Those caught in the wild seldom become tame; however, the few available today are aviary-bred. Its talent for imitation is only mediocre but this beautiful Cockatoo is primarily a subject for a large flight, where it can show off its splendour. When it is excited, it raises its crest and bows its head.

This species has often been bred in aviaries. Natural tree trunks or stout oak barrels can be used as nest boxes. In one case, the barrel was fixed 1.5 m (2 ft) above ground on scaffolding and the entrance hole was lined with metal. The interior was lined at the base with peat. Four eggs were laid, one a day on alternate days. The female incubated by day and the male by night, for a total of twenty-one or twenty-two days. They both fed the young. After some two months, the young were fledged. Rearing food is the same as for the Rose-breasted Cockatoo. Leadbeater's Cockatoo does not require heat during winter.

Cockatiels (*Nymphicus*)

Cockatiel (*N. hollandicus*) (illustrated p. 42)

Characteristics: 33 cm (13 in) long. Male—slate grey; yellow head; orange ear patch; secondaries white; undertail coverts black. Female—grey-yellow head; ear patch duller than male's; secondaries grey-white; greyish-white transverse stripes on undertail coverts. Young—similar to female. Young males often have fewer small white speckles on the underside of the wing, young females, more and larger speckles. It is sometimes possible to spot more intensive colouring on head and ear coverts of young males, even when they are still in the nest box. The upper tail feather is a uniform grey, whereas the female's is more marbled. The moult into adult plumage is usually complete by nine months.

Origin and habit: Australian interior. This species lives on the open savannah and grasslands. A pair remain together throughout the year, even when they are flying in large flocks. Their habitats are often subject to drought, giving rise to a shortage of food. So it is quite common to see large flocks undertaking lengthy migrations in order to find seeds of grasses, crops and weeds, as well as water. This is a common bird in Australia; it nests in dead eucalyptus trees. I was able to observe that many of the entrance holes were so narrow that the bird could hardly turn round. In the wild, Cockatiels are so shy that it is difficult to photograph them. Their flight is very rapid.

General remarks: There is much to be said in favour of the Cockatiel. Along with Budgerigars and Lovebirds, Cockatiels are very common cage birds in Europe. They are hardy, undemanding, easy to breed and tolerant of other species. In the house they are tame, affectionate and loving. You can always find one in a dealer's shop at a very reasonable price. The shrill whistling of a male in breeding condition could get on the nerves of the more sensitive owner after a while.

Food: Canary seed, sunflower, oats (both with and without husks), millet, chopped carrot, apples, chickweed, plantains and other weeds. Offer fresh twigs for chewing. When breeding: germinated millet sprays or oats, soaked white bread or rolls are all good supplements.

Housing and rearing. In the house: A Cockatiel needs a cage that is at least 50 cm (1 ft 8 in) long. It is a very active bird with a long, beautiful tail. It tries to occupy itself by walking about and by nibbling everything in sight. It is a rapid and enthusiastic flyer and should be allowed an exercise period in the living room at least once a day. It is best to start off with a young male because the females are less easily tamed. In addition, you have more chance of success in teaching a young male to sing a little melody or say a few words. Should you ever get the very rare opportunity of acquiring a hand-reared bird, do not miss it for such a bird becomes as tame as a dog, and craves the company of humans. Its favourite perch is your shoulder. It likes to be up high, nestling snugly in your hair. Any necklaces run the risk of being undone. This pet is intensely interested in anything which gleams or glistens, or is chewable. Even the smallest piece of wood keeps him busy for hours, but do not allow him access to the heads of matches, which are poisonous!

Young Cockatiels, and even some adults, prove easy to tame. One particular Cockatiel from a flight was wild, and bit so fiercely that it drew blood from my fingers. In order to tame it I—reluctantly—clipped some 3 cm (1¼ in) from one wing. He instinctively realized that he could no longer escape from people. One evening I wrapped him in a light silk cloth with only his head showing, and held him in my lap. I spoke softly to him as he was fed titbits of rusk crumbs, apple and carrots. At first very shy, he eventually accepted the offerings. Only a few hours later, this bird was a changed character. He was relaxed and calm, no longer bit, but merely nibbled my fingers gently. He allowed me to take him in my hand and caress him—in short, he was fully tamed. Now he was allowed to spend the whole day running up and down his favourite windowsill. His clipped feathers grew back completely after the full moult and he was able to fly again. However, he remained tame.

In the garden: A Cockatiel can endure any degree of cold in winter and you can leave him in his flight and unheated shelter without a moment's hesitation. The smallest flight should be not less than 2 m long, 1 m wide and 2 m high (6 ft 6 in × 3 ft 3 in × 6 ft 6 in). Cockatiels belong to the most successful breeders of all tame parrots. Take care not to build the nest box too small—internal dimensions of about 35–40 cm × 20 cm ($13\frac{3}{4}$–$15\frac{3}{4}$ × 8 in) should be about right, the diameter of the entrance hole should be 8–9 cm (3–$3\frac{1}{2}$ in). A pair can raise two or three broods, each of four to seven young, in a year. On no account allow more, as this weakens the birds. Incubation takes eighteen or nineteen days. The cock bird sits from early morning to late afternoon and the female takes care of the remainder. The young are fledged in four or five weeks but continue to be fed by the parents until they are about two months old. It takes about three months for the flesh-coloured beak to take on its permanent dark hue. Full moult is achieved at nine months, at which time the male displays his black tail feathers and his beautiful sulphur-yellow crest. Once fully moulted, birds may breed, although this does not always succeed during the first year of life.

Cockatiels are peace-loving birds and never cause any upset to any other bird in the flight. It is possible to keep them together with Budgerigars. *Mutations:* Albinos were bred in 1959 in America. This mutation has become very popular and you can buy albinos at favourable prices. In addition, you can get pied Cockatiels, Pearl specimens and several other mutations. Over the years, the male loses his 'pearling' but Pieds and other mutations retain the coloration throughout their lives.

Patterns of heredity in albinos:

1,0 albino × 0,1 albino = albino male and albino female
1,0 albino × 0,1 normal = split-gene male and albino female
1,0 normal × 0,1 albino = split-gene male and normal female
1,0 split-gene × 0,1 albino = albino male and albino female and split-gene male and normal female
1,0 split-gene × 0,1 normal = split-gene male and albino female and normal male and normal female

White Cockatiels have no external sex characteristics. You can only sex them according to their song or their pattern of heredity. Likewise, a split bird is visually no different from a normal one. A female cannot be split for albino or any other sex-linked colour.

White Cockatiels with black eyes do not transmit genes according to their sex:

white × white = 100% white
white × normal = 100% normal/split
white × normal/split = 50% white
50% normal/split
normal/split × normal/split = 25% white
25% normal
50% normal/split

Polytelis parrakeets

Princess of Wales Parrakeet *P. alexandrae*
Barraband Parrakeet *P. swainsonii*
Rock Pebbler *P. anthopeplus*

This Australian genus is characterized by the long tail feathers, the longest of which is the centre one. Their beaks are reddish.

Princess of Wales Parrakeet (*P. alexandrae*) (illustrated p. 42)

Characteristics: 38 cm (15 in) long. Male—brow and upper head grey-blue; neck, back and upper tail coverts olive; lower back and rump blue; chin and throat pink; wings bright green; there is an upward-curving tip to the third primary, sometimes called a spatula; red beak. Female—slate coloured brow; wing coverts narrower and more olive green; lower back slate blue; tail shorter than male's and no curl at tip of third primary; beak a duller red. Young—as female but duller. Young males often show broader, brighter green in the wings and blue on the lower back. They are fully coloured at around ten or twelve months. The blue head feathers come through first in the males.

Origin and habit: Australian interior. This species inhabits the dry grassland plains, feeding off various grass seeds. As a result, it spends much of its time on the ground and when in danger, attempts to escape by running. When hunting for food it remains very quiet, whereas when it is in the trees, it is always calling. It slinks, reptile-like, along the branches for camouflage. Like the Cockatiel, Bourke's Parrakeet and Budgerigar, this species migrates in dry conditions to find better habitats. It nests in hollow branches along the banks of rivers which only carry water at particular times, so incubation varies according to weather conditions and is not linked to the seasons. It is common to find several pairs in one area at breeding time.

General remarks: This pale pastel Parrakeet is a much sought after aviary subject. It was still quite a rarity around 1960, but nowadays it is found in aviaries everywhere. The Princess of Wales Parrakeet is never wild or shy and willingly eats from the hand. Males are commoner than females.

Food: Millet, canary seed, corn, oats and some sunflower seeds; also, all weed seeds and other seedlings, which can be left to sprout in the ground; apples, carrots and plenty of chickweed. When breeding, feed plenty of small seeds, which can be left to sprout, chopped up hard boiled egg or other soft food and any wild plants.

Housing and rearing: Do not keep this Parrakeet in a cage on account of its long tail feathers. Hand-reared birds become very tame.

In the garden: The flight must be 4 m (13 ft) or more long so that the long tail feathers can be shown to advantage. Since this is not a wood chewing species, its house can be of wood and the shelter need not be heated—not even a temperature of −25°C (−13°F) upsets it. You need an earth floor so that you can germinate seeds in it.

It would be possible to keep two pairs in a very large aviary, as long as you provided enough nest sites. They have been kept happily with Bourke's Parrakeets and Cockatiels. However, breeding with only one pair is more straightforward and usually more successful. They are not particularly choosy about nest sites—they have bred in holes measuring from 50 or 60 cm long to 2 m (1 ft 8 in or 2 ft to 6 ft 6 in). Place the boxes on a slope because the female is then less likely to drop down on the eggs and break them. The base of the nest box needs to be about 23 cm sq (9½ in sq) and the entrance hole 9 cm (3½ in) across.

The display of the male is very interesting. He hops and dances round the female on the floor of the aviary, all the while trying to feed her as he twists his head this way and that. It is noticeable that, while this is going on, the pupils of his eyes are very narrow, almost mere slits. The females lay very soon afterwards, in March or April, usually four to six eggs, which they then incubate for eighteen to twenty days. During this period, the male feeds his mate. The fledglings come out of the nest at about five weeks.

Young cocks begin their mating display as early as the autumn of their first year, also exhibiting that peculiar narrowing of the pupils. Generally speaking, Princess of Wales Parrakeets are mature at around two years of age, but successful breeding has been known to take place earlier. Nor is it unusual to get two broods in one year.

Mutations: In 1951 and 1962 blue mutations were reported in Australia, of which there is a small stock in Europe. In 1975 the first Lutinos were bred in Halle, in the German Democratic Republic, by D. Meyer.

Barraband Parrakeet (*P. swainsonii*) (illustrated p. 53)

Characteristics 37 to 40 cm (14½–15¾ in) long. Male—green; front of head, cheeks and upper throat yellow; lower throat red; beak red; iris yellow-brown. Female—green, no yellow; iris brown. Young—green, sexes similar, though males sometimes have pale yellowish tint above and below beak and brighter green on head. Young males begin to twitter after a few months and occasionally a few red or yellow feathers are visible soon afterwards. At around six months sexes are distinguishable by colour of iris. They are fully coloured between twelve and fifteen months.

Origin and habit: Inland in New South Wales and northern Victoria. The Barraband Parrakeet is the most geographically restricted of the Australian Parrakeets but where it exists, it is very common. In the dry areas, it chooses to live near riverbeds but where there is more water available, it feels free to

Barraband Parrakeets: *left*, male; *right*, female.

nest anywhere. It, too, likes the tall eucalyptus trees. During the breeding season, the Barraband flies in flocks. You find its eggs in high, hollow branches, not far from rivers.

They find their food on the ground—seeds of various grasses, purple medick, shepherd's purse, thistles and, in the cultivated regions, wheat.

General remarks: Barrabands are not as trusting as Princess of Wales Parrakeets. Sometimes, they suffer from traumatic paralysis in the leg, which seldom recovers. The feet of an affected bird become clenched in such a way that it can no longer sit. During the breeding season, their voices are heard mainly in the mornings and evenings. They are in the same price range as the Princess of Wales. Likewise, more males than females are available.

Food: Sunflower, canary seed, oats, wheat, millet, wild plants, apples, carrots and chickweed. When breeding, add germinating seeds and soft foods.

Housing and rearing. In the house: Barrabands are really aviary subjects. They have shown imitative and whistling talents.

In the garden: If you intend to breed them, your birds will need an aviary measuring at least 4 m (13 ft). In aviaries which are too small, the eggs may be infertile. The females prefer large, tree-like nest boxes, but they have been known to use 50 cm (1 ft 8 in) deep, natural-looking boxes. These should always be placed in the inner shelter and have a base measuring 25 cm sq (10 in sq). The male displays by leaping round and round the female, raising his crest and spreading his wings. It is quite common for this to go on for several weeks before eggs are laid.

The female lays from four to six eggs, one every two days. After the second one has been laid, they are incubated for nineteen to twenty days. If you wish to supervise the nest, be very careful because many females resent inspection. When they are five weeks old, the young leave the nest but are fed by their parents for a further four weeks. It is quite safe to leave the brood with the parents until the next breeding season, though, as a rule, only one brood is reared. A female is mature at one year but a male is not ready for breeding until the age of two or three. Barraband Parrakeets are hardy enough to overwinter outdoors without heating. They are not great wood nibblers. They may also be kept with other Parrakeets outside the breeding season.

Rock Pebbler (*P. anthopeplus*) (illustrated p. 55)

Characteristics: 40 cm (15¾ in) long. Male—yellow-olive; outer wing feathers and tail black; greenish back; middle secondaries and some of the large wing coverts are red; lower back and rump are yellow; beak red and iris brown. Female—olive green; inner edge of tail feathers pink; surface of tail feathers dark green; beak a dull red. Young—as female. Sometimes the males are distinguished by a slightly more yellowish tinge. Some six or eight months after hatching, yellow feathers appear on the head and breast of males. They are fully coloured between fifteen and eighteen months, but the colouring becomes even more intensive during the following year.

Origin and habit: South-east and south-west Australia. At one time, a drought led to the formation of a desert, which had the effect of dividing this bird's territory into two. The species has not yet become two distinct races, although the south-eastern version has a predominantly yellow colouring, whereas that in the south-west is much greener. Some thirty years ago, the eastern Rock Pebbler had almost died out, but now it is more common again in some parts. The exact opposite was the case in the south-west—it took advantage of the vast wheat plains and increased tremendously in numbers. Here it is found in large numbers but always splits up into small groups, never being found in huge flocks. When I was in Western Australia, I was able to observe them feeding on the wheat crop. Some were flying only a metre above ground level at great speed and I could only identify them by their voices. They also look for insects and nectar in the blossoms of the eucalyptus trees. On the ground they search for ears of wheat and grass seeds.

Rock Pebbler (male). Rock Pebblers are splendid birds, well suited to the aviary.

They breed in very high trees, often having the actual nest several metres lower than the entrance hole. Breeding takes place any time between August and December.

General remarks: The Rock Pebbler is the largest of the Parrakeets. People prefer the yellowish form because it looks more beautiful than the green. Unfortunately, this bird is prone to traumatic paralysis. One evening you can be admiring its beautiful appearance; next morning you find it lying on its belly, unable to move its legs. This phenomenon has most probably been caused by fright, such as the presence of a tawny owl or a cat.

Females are harder to come by than males.

Feeding: Sunflower seed, partially ripened corn on the cob, canary seed, oats (with and without husks), millet, especially spray millet, dandelions and other wild plants. At breeding time, add chopped up hard-boiled egg, a few meal beetle larvae or pupae, plenty of carrots, sprouted seeds and weed seeds.

Housing and rearing: Keeping the Pebbler in a cage in the house is not recommended, despite the fact that it is kept like that in its homeland. It will imitate words and can become very tame.

In the garden: The flight should not be less than 5 m (16 ft 6 in) long as the birds will then be more willing to breed. Pebblers do not destroy wood, so no particularly strong construction material will be required. Fairly deep nest boxes—1–1.5 m (3 ft 3 in–5 ft)—are best as they most closely resemble the natural sites. The floor should be 25 cm (10 in) across and the entrance hole 9 cm (3½ in).

As with all Parrakeets, the female of the species begs food from the male. She lays four to six eggs in April or May and incubates them for three weeks. The male feeds her both in the flight and on the nest. The young are fledged at six or seven weeks and are very nervous at first. As a rule, they are mature at two or three years of age.

Crimson-winged Parrakeets (*Aprosmictus*)

Crimson-winged Parrakeet *A. erythropterus* (2 races)
Timor Island Crimson-winged Parrakeet *A. jonquillaceus* (2 races)

Origin and habit: Australia, New Guinea, Timor and Wetar islands. In the wild, the Crimson-winged Parrakeet lives in small groups, but it is often found in huge flocks after the breeding season has ended. It is said to be an unforgettable picture when hundreds of these birds are spotted perching in the branches of the blossom-covered acacia trees. They are mainly fruit eaters, particularly keen on berries, the fruits of the wild passion flowers and partially ripened seeds of Sudan grass. They breed in the hollows of the giant eucalyptus trees.

General remarks: The Crimson-winged Parrakeet is among the most popular of Parrakeets. As recently as the early 1960s, they were considered as rarities, but nowadays they are continually offered for sale by devotees. Most popular of all is the larger race from the interior and south of Australia, which has a black back. Birds from the other regions are smaller and their backs are more dark grey to grey-black.

Crimson-wings are among the hardiest of birds, and those bred here can safely be left outdoors even in the lowest of temperatures without coming to any harm. They will let themselves be snowed under, rather than seek shelter.

Feeding: Sunflower, canary seed, millet, including sprays, some hemp, apples, carrots, chickweed, dandelion leaves and, for breeding, additional germinated seeds of all types, chopped up hard-boiled egg and softened stale white bread.

Housing and rearing: The Crimson-winged Parrakeet is an aviary subject. Some birds can become very tame and trusting.

In the garden: This large bird needs a flight of about 5 m (16 ft 6 in) in length where it can show off its splendid colours and get enough wing exercise. Since it eats only fresh twigs, the aviary and shelter can safely be built of wood. Nor need the wire netting be especially strong.

This species must be kept in separate pairs during the breeding season, but at other times it can be housed with other species. If you put two pairs side by side in adjoining aviaries, you may find that breeding is not always successful.

Males are generally not mature until their third year, females at two years. With some Crimson-winged Parrakeets, the problem at breeding time may well be the choice of nest site. At one time, I had six different sites in the aviary for two of my pairs because the females could not make up their minds to stick to one place—they simply dropped their eggs wherever they happened to be. Finally, in the fourth year, one of them settled on a high beech trunk inside the inner shelter, and the other went for the space behind an oak log on the floor, also in the interior. This just goes to show how contrary Crimson-wings can be. There is no such thing as a norm. I have also heard that these birds prefer to breed in the open flights, some say in normal nest boxes, others say in very tall tree trunks some 2 m (6 ft 6 in) high. On another occasion, they bred in an orange box which was intended for some bantams. So, it is imperative that you offer your birds several types of nest

Left: Young Crimson-winged Parrakeets in the nest.

Right: Timor Island Crimson-winged Parrakeet.

sites, both inside and outside the inner shelter. They like an entrance hole measuring some 9–10 cm (3½–4 in) in diameter.

The male becomes very lively in March or April, pursuing his mate with chirruping calls. When mating is imminent, he flutters his wings, all the time uttering a 'twee-twee' call, and finally the female solicits food from him. As early as April two to four eggs are laid, which the female then incubates for nineteen to twenty-two days. It is unusual for more than three young to survive. The male feeds the female for ten to fourteen days and then takes over the task of feeding the young when the female has left the nest. They are fledged at about six weeks but are still fed by the male for a further four weeks. A second clutch is very rare. On warm days in autumn you may observe a repeat mating display but it never comes to anything.

The first moult is between March and July of the first year and often hinders breeding. As the years go by, however, this gradually shifts to the summer months, so that in the third year moulting is over by July.

Crimson-winged Parrakeet (*A. erythropterus erythropterus*) east Australia, south Queensland and New South Wales (illustrated pp. 42 and 57)

Characteristics: 34 cm (13½ in) long. Male—leaf green; back and shoulders black; wing covers scarlet; rump blue; iris red-brown; beak reddish. Female—green; rump blue; slight red edging to wing covers; beak flesh-coloured. Young—as female but with black iris. Males develop their first black back feathers at around eighteen months; full mature plumage at three years. Sometimes you can only distinguish the sexes by comparing the shape of the heads, undertail coverts and wing coverts of several specimens.

New Guinea Crimson-winged Parrakeet (*A. erythropterus coccineopterus*) south New Guinea, northern Australia—Arnhemland and Kimberley

Characteristics: 32 cm (12½ in) long. Male—wing coverts bright red; back and shoulders grey-black.

Timor island Crimson-winged Parrakeet (*A. jonquillaceus jonquillaceus*) Island of Timor (illustrated p. 57)

Characteristics: 30 cm (12 in) long. Male—only front wing coverts are red, rear ones yellow; underside of tail feathers black, with yellow edging to the longest ones; no black on back. Female—inner tail feathers have yellow edging. Young—olive green; lower back turquoise; very little red in the wings. After the moult, males acquire additional yellow feathers in their wings.

Wetar Island Crimson-winged Parrakeet (*A. jonquillaceus wetterensis*)
Island of Wetar

Characteristics: Wing coverts have only minimal red with some yellow; a smaller bird.

King Parrakeets (*Alisterus*)

Australian King Parrakeet *A. scapularis* (2 races)
Green-winged King Parrakeet *A. chloropterus* (3 races)
Amboina King Parrakeet *A. amboinensis* (5 races)

Origin and habit: Australia, New Guinea, Seram, Ambon, Halmahera and neighbouring small islands. The majestic King Parrakeet lives in wooded and thickly planted regions, some on the coasts and others in the mountains. They eat mainly fruits, berries and seeds but in farming areas they converge in huge flocks on the maize fields. Since they are not hunted, they know no fear of man. They even share food bowls with the poultry on the larger farms.

The female lays four to six eggs in the hollow branches or trunks of giant eucalyptus trees.

General remarks: Many breeders feel that this is the ideal bird; it is large but undemanding and some have been kept for thirty-one years—and in the last season, the female even laid fertile eggs! They are quarrelsome among themselves but tolerant with other species out of the breeding season.

Feeding: Sunflower, oats, some hemp, maize, millet, carrots, apples, other fruits and chickweed. Offer soaked stale white bread or rusks, chopped up hard-boiled egg, freshly gathered weed seeds, rowanberries, hips, and so on, at breeding time.

Housing and rearing: The King Parrakeet is not a suitable cage bird.

In the garden: An aviary for a King Parrakeet should be some 6 m long, 2 m high and 1 m wide (19 ft 10 in × 6 ft 6 in × 3 ft 3 in) and the ground area of the shelter should be 4 m sq (13 ft sq). Do not put many branches in the flight because they will restrict the bird's flying. It is possible to have a wooden aviary because the King Parrakeet does not chew wood. An acclimatized bird, or one bred in this country, needs no heating in winter because it is impervious to frost. These birds are not easy to breed. You need to offer them several nesting sites of a variety of types, though they tend to prefer hollow logs with a depth of 1–2 m (3 ft 3 in–6 ft 6 in), a breadth at the base of 30 cm (1 ft) and a 10 cm (4 in) wide entrance hole. The female begs food from the male at breeding time. If he feeds her, there is more chance of a successful mating. If you have had no success with a pair by the third year, all you can do is change the partners, as the pair may not be compatible.

The male raises his head feathers and spreads his wings jerkily whilst uttering strange noises during the mating display. The female lays four to six eggs and incubates them for nineteen to twenty-one days. The young leave the nest at about six weeks. Males are mature at three years, females usually at about two, which is also when they have their full plumage. Australian King Parrakeets (*A. scapularis*) have been crossed with Green-winged King Parrakeets, Crimson-winged Parrakeets and also with Barraband Parrakeets.

Australian King Parrakeet (*A. scapularis*) south Queensland, New South Wales and Victoria (illustrated p. 43)

Characteristics: 40 cm (15¾ in) long. Male—head and underparts brilliant red; shoulders green; rump and band on nape blue; back and wings dark green; beak reddish; iris yellow. Female—green; belly red; rump blue; beak grey-black; iris yellow-brown. Young—as female but beak yellower. Young females often develop a darker beak, particularly on the upper side, after a few months. Males show their first red feathers on the head and breast after some twelve months and are fully moulted by three years.
Mutations: When I was in Denmark, I saw photographs of yellow King Parrakeets.

Green-winged King Parrakeet (*A. chloropterus*) South-east New Guinea (illustrated p. 43)

Characteristics: 37 cm (14½ in) long. Male—plumage almost totally a harsh bright green/yellow; head and underparts darker red. Female—dark blue rump; undertail feathers blue with reddish edging. Young—no red on breast and undertail coverts, beak pale horn colour.
This species is still very rare in confinement and there can only be a few examples in Europe. I did see a pair in San Diego Zoo, California, and there are several in England.

Amboina King Parrakeet (*A. amboinensis*) Islands of Ambon and Ceram (illustrated p. 43)

Characteristics: Wings green, rump blue, all other plumage red; upper beak red with a black tip; lower beak black. Female—smaller head and beak; edges of smaller wing feathers are red. Young—covered in black down in the nest; when fledged, have white eye rings; plumage otherwise as adults. After initial problems with acclimatization, there are now some very hardy colonies which can happily withstand several degrees of frost. They need plenty of fruit in the winter, particularly oranges, also berries and maize, to keep their vitamin intake balanced. The best idea is to deep freeze several types of food in the autumn, ready for winter feeding. This beautiful King Parrakeet was first bred in Switzerland in 1974, in Germany in 1975 by P. Schauf of Cologne, and in 1976 H. Dörffer of Norderstedt raised three young and K. Eckardt of Hamburg-Schenefeld raised one. Each clutch contained three eggs at the most. This King Parrakeet will use a nest box measuring anything from 60 cm to 180 cm (2 ft–6 ft), in June or July. At first, the young are naked, then grow a black down. The eye ring remains white. One pair bred in the fourth year after being imported from Indonesia. In the mornings and evenings, their voices are somewhat loud and screechy; by contrast, their mating call is pleasantly flute-like.

Pileated Parrakeets (*Purpureicephalus*)

Pileated Parrakeet (*P. spurius*)

Characteristics: 37 cm (14½ in) long. Male—upper head red, other upper plumage green; cheeks yellow-green; breast and belly violet; centre rump and undertail coverts red; beak horn-grey. Female—smaller head than male, not always with definite red top (sometimes just a few red feathers, sometimes reddish-brown cap); underside a washed-out blue. Some females look just like the males. Shortly before leaving the nest, a young female has several patches of scattered white spots on the underside of the flight feathers, whereas the young male only has one patch, of about six spots which he loses later; head green with a small red stripe on the brow; adult plumage at around one year.

Origin and habit: South-west Australia. The Pileated Parrakeet is at home in the vast eucalyptus forests because its main source of food is the eucalyptus seed. It takes them from the tree as well as from the ground, holding them in its feet. It is helped by its very long upper mandible. On a trip to Western Australia during November I observed some unripe fruits that had been chewed by the birds. Pileated Parrakeets also take the nectar from flowers and other fruit, thus, they are a great nuisance to the apple growers. In the orchards they are the second most common Parrakeet and can do much damage. They always fly around in small groups, never in huge flocks.

The female breeds in very high hollow trees or branches where she lays a large clutch, often five to seven eggs at a time, and sometimes even nine. Breeding takes place during the autumn, the young remaining with their parents for a very long time afterwards. They keep to the 50–70 m (55–77 yd) high trees, where they are difficult to spot.

General remarks: The Pileated Parrakeet is no longer a rarity as it is now bred regularly. However, it is often rejected in favour of other species, despite its beautiful plumage, because it is extremely shy. Hand-reared birds give the

61

most pleasure. One fancier in Australia had birds which were so tame that they would fly on to his head or shoulder and take titbits from his hand.

Feeding: Sunflower, oats or groats, wheat, canary seed, berries, peanuts, plenty of apples and fresh green twigs for chewing; at breeding time, additional apples, chickweed, and soaked rusks.

Housing and rearing: Because of its very shy nature, only a hand-reared bird could be kept in the house.

In the garden: The longest aviary you can possibly manage is essential for this Parrakeet. Avoid a wooden construction as they chew everything (even when you give them plenty of fresh green twigs specifically for this purpose). There is no need to heat the shelter in winter as they are insensitive to low temperatures. Pileated Parrakeets have been known to breed as early as one year of age. Their favourite nestbox is a natural log about 50 cm (1 ft 8 in) deep with an entrance hole of 8–9 cm (3–3½ in). The male has a very idiosyncratic display: he raises his head feathers and spreads his tail feathers, lifting them over his back as he dangles his wings. In this attitude he approaches his female. She lays four to seven eggs and incubates them for twenty-four days. The male regurgitates food for her and both parents feed the young. They are fledged at about five weeks but fed by their parents for many weeks more.

The female is extremely sensitive to disturbance during incubation and abandons the nest immediately if she is disturbed. A pair should be housed in a quiet situation if possible. There are many breeders who remove the eggs as soon as they are laid and give them to another species (Redrump Parrakeet, Barraband) to incubate but this leads to new problems when they are fledged, as they then no longer receive food from their foster-parents. Your only alternative then is to hand feed them. Such birds obviously become very trusting and tame and are very suitable as potential breeding birds.

Rosellas *(Platycercus)*

Green Rosella/Yellow-bellied rosella *P. caledonicus*
Crimson Rosella/Pennants Parrakeet *P. elegans* (3 races)
Adelaide Rosella *P. adelaidae*
Yellow Rosella *P. flaveolus*
Red Rosella (Golden-mantled Rosella) *P. eximius* (3 races)
Blue Rosella/Mealy Rosella *P. adscitus* (2 races)
Stanley Rosella/Western Rosella *P. icterotis* (2 races)
Brown's Rosella *P. venustus*

All types in this genus are very closely related. Their territories border, and even overlap, each other, which is why hybrids occur, even in the wild. They are all very brightly coloured, with broad scalloped tails and black edging to their back feathers.

Green Rosella/Yellow-bellied Rosella (*P. caledonicus*)

Characteristics: 36 cm (14 in) long. Male—larger than female; red brow; blue cheek patches and wing coverts; rest of head and underparts matt yellow; green rump. Female—smaller and often narrower head; red brow band; underparts somewhat paler; whole appearance more fragile. Young—still green during whole of first year, final plumage at about sixteen months. Sexes differentiated by relative sizes of head, beak and body. Females always have a darker beak.

Origin and habit: Tasmania and surrounding islands. Green Rosellas are predominant in the north and north-east of the island, where they prefer the less dense woodland. They take nectar from the blossoms of the eucalyptus trees, as well as a variety of berries and seeds, also rose-hips and insects and their larvae.

It breeds in the hollows of very high branches where the female lays five to eight eggs in December. They are not a protected species because they cause heavy damage to crops.

General remarks: Take care to acquire pure-bred birds, though there will, of course, be some natural colour variations.

Birds from the east and the interior of Tasmania are more brightly coloured than those from the west. The latter are more olive green and have small blue markings on their wings.

The Green Rosella is not only the largest but also the hardiest of its genus. It is used to snow and ice. Its whole appearance is stocky, having a stout body and short tail feathers.

Feeding: Sunflower, oats and groats, canary seed, millet, carrots, rose hips and hawthorn berries, plantains and partially-ripe corn. At breeding time, feed additional carrots with chopped up hard-boiled egg and ground rusk and softened stale white bread.

Housing and rearing: The Green Rosella is an aviary subject, not at all suitable for the house.

In the garden: You can safely keep this bird in an unheated flight and shelter, since it is a very hardy subject. Unlike other Parrakeets, this one breeds either very early in the year or in late spring. P. Woelken in Hamburg even reported eggs in February—eight of them—and a second clutch at the end of May, and that was with young birds which had not even acquired their full adult plumage at the time! The eggs were incubated for about twenty days by the female, who was fed by the male the whole time. The nest was built on a base measuring some 25 cm (10 in) across and in a box about 45–80 cm (17¾–32 in) deep, with an entrance hole of some 8 cm (3 in) diameter. Four to

63

seven youngsters are the norm and it is best to leave them with their parents for as long as you can.

When the Green Rosella refused to rear her young, they were handed over to Stanley Parrakeets or Red-fronted Parrakeets and this can work.

Crimson Rosella (*P. elegans*) (illustrated p. 43)

Characteristics: 33–36 cm (13–14 in) long. Male—crimson; cheeks, tail and wings predominantly blue; back feathers black with red edges; strong beak and sturdy head. Female—smaller head and narrower beak. Young—from completely green to almost red. Adult plumage at thirteen to fifteen months. *Origin and habit:* Coastal regions of east and south Australia. Crimson Rosellas inhabit the vast woodland areas which, unfortunately, are disappearing under vast clearance schemes. Consequently, their numbers are diminishing. The northern species lives in very hot zones, whereas the southern one endures frost and snow in winter and has even been found at 2000 m. They feed on seeds of the eucalyptus trees, berries, fruits and, to some extent, insects. They also pick up seeds from the ground. They breed in very high branches of hollow trees, where they lay from four to eight eggs. There is sometimes a second brood in the autumn of a damp year. Much has already been written about 'crimson' and 'green' Rosellas. The 'small crimson Rosella' (*P. elegans nigrescens*) lives in the warm north of Australia, whereas the 'large green Rosella' (*P. elegans elegans*) inhabits the south-east. The former leaves the nest in its almost totally red plumage and the larger species emerges completely green. Where both types overlap, mixed colouring is common. A third race, *P. elegans melanoptera*, lives on the southern Kangaroo Island.
General remarks: The Crimson Rosella is extraordinarily popular with breeders. It has a not unpleasant voice which is really only noticeable during the breeding season. It soon gets used to you and will happily feed from your hand. Males in particular soon become tame.

On occasion, it has been noticed that their plumage deteriorates—probably due to vitamin deficiency, or some other feeding imbalance. It is particularly noticeable on the underside, where the feathers take on a greyish look. Only seldom is it possible to eradicate this, by offering an extremely varied diet of foods and vitamins.
Feeding: Sunflower, canary seed, sometimes oats or wheat, millet, rowanberries, rose hips, whitebeam and hawthorn berries, dandelion (both leaves and seedheads), plantains, plenty of apples, carrots and chickweed, and a regular supply of fresh green twigs to chew. At breeding time, add soaked stale white bread, rusks, chopped hard-boiled egg, germinated spray millet and chickweed.
Housing and rearing: This Parrakeet is suitable only for an aviary, despite the

fact that a hand-reared bird does become extremely tame, because, as a woodland bird, its red plumage needs a certain amount of humidity which the interior of a house lacks.

In the garden: The overall length of the flight and inner shelter should be not less than 4–5 m (13 ft–16 ft 6 in). You must construct in iron because this is one of the wood-chewing varieties, and this applies to the shelter as well. They have been known to chew through 16 mm ($\frac{1}{2}$ in) boarding. Neither is thin wire netting a good idea. It saves trouble if you take these factors into account right at the beginning. They are not troubled by cold and even bathe in fairly cold conditions.

Early in the new year, the male becomes very active as the breeding season approaches and becomes intolerant of other birds. Do not put pairs of the same species in neighbouring aviaries. You may even have to consider erecting a double layer of netting between flights. They are not fussy about nest sites and have been known to use large or small natural logs or boxes. However, the female incubates more happily and successfully in a large natural box. She lays up to eight eggs and incubates them for twenty-one to twenty-two days. The young are fledged after four or five weeks and are fed by their parents for a further two or three weeks. On occasion, a one-year-old pair have reared offspring, despite the fact that they themselves had not yet acquired their final adult plumage at the time. A second brood in the year is rare. Females are more sought after than males.

Adelaide Rosella (*P. adelaide*) (illustrated p. 44)

Characteristics: 35 cm (13$\frac{3}{4}$ in) long. Male—underside hyacinth blue; belly area paler, often with yellow tones; the black back feathers have yellow edges. Colouring is very variable because this is an intergrade species. Female—smaller head and beak. Young—olive green back; greenish underparts; head, breast and rump brick red.

Origin and habit: South Australia around the city of Adelaide. In the natural habitat these birds vary greatly. The underparts can be redder or yellower. It appears to represent a hybrid population and is found in many types of landscape. It is no longer common around the city of Adelaide. They breed in acacias and eucalyptus trees, whose seeds they eat. They also feed on berries, fruit and weed seeds.

General remarks: You do not often see this bird in captivity, perhaps due to its rather idiosyncratic colouring—breeders seem to prefer the more brightly coloured Crimson Rosella—but also, perhaps, because you cannot always be sure that you are looking at a pure-bred Adelaide Rosella.

Feeding: As Crimson Rosella.

Housing and rearing: Very little difference from the above. The female is said to be rather sensitive about being disturbed on the nest at first.

Yellow Rosella (*P. elegans flaveolus*) (illustrated below)

Characteristics: 34 cm (13½ in) long. Male—straw-coloured; cheeks, wing edges and outer tail feathers blue; red brow band; black back feathers with yellow edges. Female—head and beak smaller than male's; red brow band often less intensely coloured than the male's. Young—underparts pale yellow-green; rump olive green; upper parts olive green with only slight black markings; underwing stripes are present. Full adult plumage at about fourteen months.

Origin and habit: Australia, in southern New South Wales. The Yellow Rosella lives in the dry regions and likes to roost in the eucalyptus trees along the river banks. Other than at breeding time, they fly round in groups made up of several families.

General remarks: Unfortunately, there are not many pure-bred Yellow Rosellas available. They are very hardy and can withstand winter very well.

Feeding: As for others, above. Do not forget to provide fresh twigs for nibbling.

Yellow Rosella.

Housing and rearing: The Yellow Rosella is an amenable aviary subject. Once you get a compatible pair together, you can expect good results. They generally lay five to seven eggs, which are incubated by the female alone. The young hatch after twenty-two days and leave the nest after five weeks. You should put the chosen nestbox in the shelter.

Red Rosella (*P. eximius eximius*)

Characteristics: 32 cm (12½ in) long. Male—head, neck and upper breast red; white cheeks; green-yellow underparts; back feathers black with greeny-yellow edges; rump yellowy-green; mantle and tail feathers blue; undertail feathers red. Female—smaller head and stature than male; cheeks not such a clear white. Young—duller colours, head and neck more green than red. Young females have even less red in the head than young males.

Origin and habit: Australia: southern New South Wales, Victoria and south-east South Australia. Originally a bird of the savannahs, it has followed man into the cultivated areas and is now quite common even in the city parks. After the breeding season it goes around in family groups, sometimes even in huge flocks, searching for food—wheat, oats, grass seeds, fruits, berries, and insects. The Red Rosella can cause a great deal of damage in the apple and pear orchards.

It nests in hollow tree trunks, usually not very high ones. It has even been found nesting on the ground. It may lay up to nine eggs and two broods are normal.

General remarks: Of all *Platycercus* types, this Rosella is the most popular with fanciers. It is always available at a very reasonable price. They have been known to live twenty, or even thirty, years in an aviary and still lay fertile eggs. Their voice is pleasant.

Feeding: Sunflower, millet, apples, carrots, greenfood, rowan berries. At breeding time, soaked white bread, sprouted spray millet.

Housing and rearing. In the house: The Red Rosella has been reared successfully in a large cage. Young birds kept alone, especially males, become very tame. They learn to whistle short tunes and to say several words. A cage for one bird should be not less than 60 cm (2 ft) long, in order to give the bird enough freedom of movement. You will have to open the cage door at least once a day to give it a chance to fly around.

In the garden: The Rosella is the ideal bird for any newcomer to Parrakeet rearing. It is completely hardy and quite happy in an aviary measuring only 3 m (9 ft 9 in) in length. You can use wood because it does not nibble.

When the breeding season starts, this Rosella can be very unpleasant towards other birds, even if they are of another species. Some, however, are quite peaceable. Never put other Rosellas in neighbouring aviaries as they can be very aggressive. They are not choosy about where they breed, as long as the box is at least 40 cm (15¾ in) deep, with a base some 25 cm (10 in) across and an entrance hole of 8 cm (3½ in). They will breed in the shelter as well as in the flight. When the male becomes ready to breed he spreads his tail feathers and begins to shake them about. If he chooses a nestbox and the female follows him into it, you can be fairly certain that the pairing will be succesful. The female usually lays five or six eggs, but up to nine have been known. She lays one egg every two days and begins to sit once the third egg has arrived. They hatch after twenty-one to twenty-two days and the young leave the nest after four weeks. Only then does the male begin to feed them, having fed only the incubating female before. The young are independent after two or three weeks. Sexes tend to be equal in number.

It is quite common for Rosellas to breed successfully in their first year. However, failures should be expected with very young birds. Two broods a year are common. They are also useful as foster parents for other Parrakeets' eggs, but here, too, failures have to be reckoned with.

Tasmanian Rosella (*P. eximius diemensis*) Tasmania

Characteristics: The red on the head and breast are brighter and of greater extent on the underparts than that of *P. eximius eximius*; very large white cheek patches.

Golden-mantled Rosella (*P. eximius ceciliae*) interior of southern Queensland and New South Wales

Characteristics: Head and breast darker red; much yellow in the back; rump blue-green. Pure examples are rarely found in captivity since crossing with other subspecies of *eximius* occurs frequently.

Blue-cheeked Rosella (*P. adscitus adscitus*)

Characteristics: 30 cm (12 in) long. Male—head somewhat yellow; lower cheeks, underparts and wing edging strong blue; rump greeny-yellow; otherwise as Mealy Rosella. Female—smaller beak; rounder head. Young— duller colours, full adult plumage at around sixteen months.
Origin and habit: It is at home in northern Queensland and Cape York Peninsular, both very warm regions. Round about the town of Cairns, this bird crosses with the Mealy Rosella. It was only identified in 1955, so not much is known about the Blue-cheeked Rosella. It breeds between February and June and it likes to eat the blossoms of the Melaleuca and eucalyptus trees, as well as acacia seeds.
General remarks: This Rosella is not common in aviaries. I first heard about it from A. Preussiger in Heimbach-Weis in 1969, when two pairs came into his

possession. If you should acquire some, protect them from frost as they have not yet been bred enough in captivity to be completely hardy in our winters.
Feeding: As for Mealy Rosella.
Housing and rearing: The Blue-cheeked Rosella has often been reared in Australia but the first European success was that of A. Preussiger, referred to above. His birds sought out a nest spot which was some 40 cm deep by 30 cm wide (15¾ in × 12 in). The floor was covered by a 5 cm (2 in) deep layer of peat, four eggs were laid. They were incubated for nineteen days and the young left the nest after thirty days.

Mealy Rosella (*P. a. palliceps*) (illustrated p. 44)

Characteristics: 33 cm (13 in) long. Male—bright yellow head; whitish cheeks with blue edging below; back feathers black with golden-yellow edging; underparts are blue to pale blue; rump bluish. Female—no definite sexual dimorphism but adult females are generally paler overall and of a smaller form and head-size. Young—plumage has washed-out appearance, head olive-green with red-brown tints. Some have red feathers on the crown, which disappear after the first full moult. Full adult plumage after twelve to fifteen months.
Origin and habit: Australia: Queensland, northern New South Wales. Whole pattern of existence resembles that of the other Rosellas. It is a bird of the savannahs, which seeks its food—all types of seed—on the ground, or flies into the orchards and corn fields for fruit and grain. It also takes berries, eucalyptus seeds and insects from the large trees. It tends to nest higher up than the Red Rosella, though the actual nest platform can be lower than the entrance hole.
General remarks: Mealy Rosellas are quite common amongst breeders, although they cost more than the Red Rosella or Stanley Rosella (Western Rosella). A Mealy in adult plumage which still has red feathers in the crown is not pure. After World War II, remaining subjects were, out of necessity, crossed with Red Rosellas, and this has led to a strain that never loses its red crown. If you intend to buy Mealy Rosellas, take a look at the parents first, or get a guarantee from the vendor.

Differentiating the sexes is a great problem. It is easiest of all when the young have only just left the nest or when they are more than one year old; in between, it is very hard. It is often easier to make up your mind by comparing several birds of the same age. The voice is not unpleasant but somewhat louder than that of the Stanley or the Red Rosella.
Feeding: Sunflower seeds, oats, some hemp, millet sprays, plenty of weed seeds, chickweed, apples and carrots. At breeding time, additional corn, soaked stale white bread and increased quantities of carrots, apples and chickweed.

Housing and rearing: Like all Rosellas, young Mealys become very tame, but I have never heard of one being kept in the house. This is also a type which belongs in the aviary.

In the garden: Birds that have been bred here can safely overwinter outdoors without heating; they all need a dry, draughtproof shelter. The Mealy Rosella is more prone to wood chewing than the Stanley and the Red Rosella, but it is not as bad as the Crimson Rosella. I would not recommend the use of old or very thin wire netting.

Breeding is as for Red Rosellas. Five to eight eggs are laid early in the year and the female likes a high situation, probably because they do not like to be disturbed. This applied to one of my females. The male, on the other hand, was very trusting and took chickweed from my hand. The rule is that this species will not breed successfully until its second year. They often lay infertile eggs in the first year. Once established, two broods a year are normal.

Stanley Rosella/Western Rosella (*P. icterotis icterotis*)

Characteristics: 28 cm (11 in) long. Male—head and underparts red; cheeks dark yellow; back feathers black with green edges. Female—red brow band; head and underparts a mixture of red and green. Young—predominantly greenish, more or less red on the belly and head, cheek patch only hinted at. Young males often have stronger colouring and sturdier heads. Adult colouring around twelve to fifteen months.

Origin and habit: The Stanley or Western Rosella is a fairly common bird in its homeland of south-west Australia, although it is not so common as the Red Rosella. It follows man, coming into the gardens and wheat plantations to search for food. It also takes fruit from the orchards but since it never comes in large flocks, people leave it alone. I saw this species both in the meadows and in the tall eucalyptus trees, where it is well camouflaged. It is here that it rears its young, during our late summer season.

General remarks: This is an extremely popular bird, also known as the Scarlet Rosella, and it is only marginally dearer than the Red Rosella. It has a pleasant, flute-like quality to its unobtrusive voice. It soon becomes tame and is small enough not to require a large space to live in. It is friendly towards other species and can safely be recommended to any beginner.

Feeding: Canary seed, sunflower kernels, millet, wild bird food, linseed, oats, wheat, chickweed, dandelion heads, shepherd's purse, plantains, apples and carrots. Give the latter especially during breeding time with hard-boiled eggs and germinated seeds.

Housing and rearing: In the house: Both young and hand-reared Stanley Rosellas become extraordinarily tame and affectionate, particularly the males. They have bred successfully indoors, in a loft measuring some 3 m (9 ft 9 in) in length. Each year between four and six young were reared.

In the garden: A flight of 3 m (9 ft 9 in) in length is enough for this species and the shelter need not be heated during winter. They do not destroy wood.

Stanleys have been known to breed successfully in their first year, even before adult plumage was assumed. The female incubates her five to eight eggs for twenty days. The young leave the nest after four weeks but you have to leave them with their parents for another five weeks or more to be sure of their survival.

The females are prone to egg binding, especially during cold weather. It is a good idea to add a little cod liver oil to their food as a precautionary measure. Add vitamins during the winter months, too. Females are in greater demand than males.

Eastern Stanley Rosella (*P. icterotis xanthogenys* (subspecies)) interior of south-west Australia

Characteristics: Larger than the above, with pale yellow cheeks, red edging to back feathers and yellowish tints to the red underparts.

Brown's Rosella (*P. venustus*)

Characteristics: 29 cm (11½ in) long. Male—head black; white cheek patch; lower edge with a blue rim; back feathers black with yellow edging; underparts yellowish; undertail coverts red; underside of tail pale blue. Female—sometimes head appears to be less jet-black than males; underparts less yellow; often no apparent difference in head and beak. Young—washed-out colouring. Mature plumage at twelve to fourteen months.
Origin and habit: Australia, to the north of the Kimberley region and in the north of the Northern Territory. Brown's Rosella inhabits the savannahs and scrublands, but has also been noted in the mangrove swamps on the coast. Whereas it was once thought of as a common bird, now it is regarded as rare. There is no obvious reason to explain this, especially since the environment has not been drastically altered by man.

It feeds on seeds, fruits and berries. Its natural breeding time is during summer and it prefers very high nest sites. Cayley (Australia) says that this species only lays two or three eggs at a time. If this is so, it is unlike any of its related species and cannot be typical.
General remarks: Brown's Rosella is the rarest of the Broadtails and its price is still exceedingly high. Imported birds are very sensitive and must be very carefully and gradually acclimatized as they are used to living in a very warm zone.
Feeding: Canary seed, sunflower seeds, white millet and spray millet, oats, hemp, linseed, niger, apples, carrots and chickweed. For breeding, additional chickweed, carrots and chopped-up hard-boiled egg.

Housing and rearing. In the house: Because of its very high price, Brown's Rosella is only kept for breeding. It should be possible to rear this species in your loft as it is a winter breeder, but if you do so, it would be best to heat the loft in order to stimulate broodiness and prevent the young from huddling together and suffocating. Very rarely does it breed in August. The clutch consists of from four to seven eggs, which the female incubates for almost three weeks. After a good four weeks, the young leave the nest.

Breeding failures are very common with this species because it refuses to transfer its breeding season to our warmer months. If ever they do have eggs earlier in the year, they are mostly infertile.
In the garden: It is just as easy to keep this Rosella in an aviary in the garden. If you expect to breed successfully, make the inner shelter as big as you possibly can and heat it.

Barnardius Parrakeets

Bauer's/Port Lincoln Parrakeet *B. zonarius* (3 races)
Barnard's Parrakeet *B. barnardi* (3 races)

These birds used to be included among the Broadtails but they have such differing characteristics that it is no longer a tenable classification. The most noticeable one is the yellow neck band. In contrast to the Broadtails, their back feathers do not have a coloured edge.

Bauer's/Port Lincoln Parrakeet (*B. zonarius zonarius*)

Characteristics: 36 cm (14 in) long. Male—no red brow band; black head; broad yellow collar; upper breast dark green with a scaly appearance; belly yellow above and to the sides. Female—same colouring; head and beak smaller. Notice the display posture of the male. Young—head black-brown; other plumage with a washed-out appearance. Adult plumage between twelve and fourteen months.
Origin and habit: Central Western Australia to the Eyre Peninsular in South Australia. Bauer's Parrakeet is another hardy species which can withstand very low temperatures. It has a trusting nature and is never shy. It prefers natural log nestboxes, where four or five eggs are laid as a rule, though seven or eight have been known. The normal breeding season is during the spring. The Bauer's Parrakeets in the interior have much more splendid colouring, especially those around Mullewa in the west. The belly area is yellow and the head is fringed with green. I was there in October when the young had just left the nest. They were perching in the bush, where the eucalyptus trees were not very tall. The further south we travelled, the less intense was their

Breeding area, in Western Australia, for Bauer's Ringneck Parrakeets, Rose-breasted Cockatoos, Cockatiels, Manycolour Parrakeets and Budgerigars.

colouring. There could be no doubt that, where their territory bordered that of the Twenty-Eight Parrakeet, interbreeding was common. We actually saw a male Twenty-Eight and a female Bauer's in front of a breeding site.

General remarks: The best way of telling the sexes apart is the larger size of the male's head and beak. However, there will always be cases of doubt. The number of devotees has increased dramatically in recent years. It is a hardy bird which is never shy. It needs constant opportunities to bathe and a wire mesh that is fairly thick. Its voice is not unpleasant.

Feeding: Sunflower, canary seed, millet, some hemp, oats, peanuts, apples, carrots, soft food mixture, weeds in milk and germinated seedlings during the breeding season.

Breeding in the garden: These birds are generally mature at about two years. The male displays by spreading out his tail feathers and shaking them from side to side, and you can often see a form of dancing display as early as March. They like a nestbox which is about 1 m (3 ft 3 in) deep with a base of some 25 cm (10 in) diameter. The female incubates the four or five eggs for about twenty-one days. Only a few months after hatching, the young are almost indistinguishable from their parents.

73

Twenty-eight Parrakeet (*B. zonarius semitorquatus*)

Characteristics: 39 cm (15¼ in) long. Male—black head; red brow band; yellow collar; cheeks dark blue; breast dark green; greenish-yellow belly and green back. Female—smaller head and beak than male; less intense black to the head; yellow collar narrower and paler than males'; and red brow band also often less pronounced. Young—paler colours. Sexes differentiated while still in the nest or shortly after leaving it by the smaller size of the beak. Young males are larger than young females.

Origin and habit: Australia, mainly in the south-west coastal region. It is the commonest species in the area, so receives no protection. They converge on the gardens, orchards and grain fields in small flocks, where they can cause great damage. They also consume weed seeds, leaf buds and unripe seeds of the eucalyptus trees. You even see them eating various flower buds or congregating in flocks in King's Park in Perth. You can get quite close to them. Twenty-eights stay paired, even outside the breeding season. They like to nest high up in the trees. The female takes care of the incubation of the five to seven eggs while the male stays on guard nearby. The youngsters stay by their parents for a very long time.

General remarks: Recently, Twenty-eights have become more common amongst breeders. It is the peculiar call with gives it the name of Twenty-eight Parrakeet. Females are in greater demand than males.

Feeding: Oats and groats, wheat, sunflower, canary seeds, millet, carrots, apples, chickweed, dandelions and rowan berries. For breeding: plenty of greenfood, sprouting seeds, chopped-up hard-boiled eggs, and stale moistened white bread.

Housing and rearing: The Twenty-eight is an aviary bird. In its homeland, it is often reared by hand and tamed. Many of them imitate words and learn to whistle (I observed this for myself in Australia—one bird whistled a tune and repeated a number of words).

In the garden: The flight should be at least 5 m (16 ft 6 in) long. Never use wood or a thin wire netting because its beak will ruin them very quickly. Twenty-eights can tolerate winter weather so no heating is necessary.

This bird has a very interesting mating display; it has even been known to turn somersaults on the ground. *B. z. occidentalis* is not dealt with here.

Barnard's Parrakeet (*B. barnardi barnardi*)

Characteristics: 33 cm (13 in) long. Male—dark red brow band; head brownish-green; yellow collar; upper parts greeny-blue; cheeks pale blue; underparts green and belly yellowish. Female—duller head colours and head smaller and narrower than male's. Young—washed-out colouring; no yellow on underparts. Adult plumage appears between twelve and fourteen months.

Origin and habit: Interior of New South Wales and Queensland. Barnard's Parrakeet inhabits the savannahs and eucalyptus bushland, avoiding the plantations and only rarely being found on farms. It has become quite rare in some areas. Its food consists of all kinds of seeds, fruits, berries, nectar and termites. It also takes the seeds and flower buds of the eucalyptus tree. Between August and November it lays from four to six eggs in hollows, high in the trees.

General remarks: The Barnard's Parrakeet is no longer a rarity.

Feeding: Sunflower, wheat, oats, canary seed, millet, apples, carrots, rowan berries, rose hips and chickweed. At breeding time: germinated seeds or partially ripe weed seeds.

Housing and rearing: They are occasionally reared by hand in their homeland, when they become very tame and learn to sing tunes.

In the garden: A pair should be housed in a flight measuring at least 4 m (13 ft) in length. It is best to avoid a wooden structure.

Birds which have been bred here can withstand our winters. Rearing them is not easy and often requires much patience. Incubation takes twenty-one to twenty-two days and the young leave the nest after four or five weeks.

Cloncurry Parrakeet (*B. barnardi macgillivrayi*) Queensland, around the town of Cloncurry

Characteristics: 32 cm (12½ in) long. Male—upper head green; no red brow band; cheeks and throat blue; yellow collar; remaining upper parts and breast green; rest of underside dark yellow; undertail feathers and wing edges blue. Female—smaller head and beak than male. Young—washed-out colouring; pale orange-yellow brow band. Mature plumage appears at thirteen to fifteen months.

Origin and habit: For a long time this species was unknown and it was not until about 1900 that the first descriptions of it were made. It has been observed both in pairs and in small groups. Like almost all Parrakeets in the drier zones, it, too, prefers to follow the course of rivers, especially those where the eucalyptus grows. It has also been seen in the woodlands, though, as well as in the bush.

General remarks: It was not available in Europe until the 1960s. You have to take into account their penchant for chewing when constructing their aviaries and steer clear of thin netting. Once they have acclimatized themselves, they are well able to take our climate. Always offer them a good supply of fresh greenery to nibble.

It is thanks to a few devoted breeders that what was once a very rare bird, is now so readily available to others.

Feeding: Sunflower, wheat, oats, canary seed, millet and millet sprays, fresh weeds and maize, apples and a variety of berries.

Breeding in the garden: Three breeders were successful for the first time in 1969. Two used nestboxes which were 40 cm (15¾ in) deep with a floor diameter of almost 30 cm (12 in), and one used a box which was 1 m (3 ft 3 in) deep. The eggs hatched after twenty days and the young left the nest between ten and twelve days later. Two broods a year are normal. They have a not unpleasant voice.

S. Australian Barnard's Parrakeet (*B. barnardi whitei*) northern South Australia

Characteristics: Upper parts dark green; orange-red brow band; otherwise as *B. barnardi barnardi.*

New Zealand Parrakeets or Kakarikis (*Cyanoramphus*)

Red-fronted Parrakeet *C. novazelandiae* (9 races)
Yellow-fronted Parrakeet *C. auriceps* (2 races)

Origin and habit: New Zealand and surrounding small islands. About a century ago, these Parrakeets were a plague on New Zealand and its neighbouring islands. Giant flocks swarmed into the plantations, wreaking havoc, and the farmers decimated them to such an extent that two races are now extinct. Others are only found on uninhabited islands. Not long ago, friends of the Red-fronted and Yellow-fronted Parrakeets sought to save them from extinction. To a large extent, they live at a latitude corresponding to that of North Germany and Denmark. They breed in the hollows of dead tree trunks, sometimes even in crevices in rocks. They feed on berries, seeds and insects. The Red-fronted Parrakeet is now a protected species.

General remarks: These Parrakeets spend much time on the floor, and they have such strong legs that they can climb horizontally up wire netting without needing to use their beaks. Another idiosyncracy is scrabbling for food with their feet when they are on the ground. They move forwards partly by hopping, another of their peculiarities. Their call is pleasant, resembling somewhat the bleating of a small goat kid. All Kakarikis have really low voices which are not in the least parrot-like. It is not their colouring but their amusing behaviour which makes them so popular. They are particularly noted for taking so many baths and for rapidly becoming so trusting.

Feeding: Sunflower, canary seed, hemp, all kinds of weeds, oats, wheat, plenty of greenfood and sprouting seeds, diced carrots and apples, berries of all types (especially rowan berries), buds from fruit trees; and in the breeding season, ready-made dried egg or your own egg mixture with soaked stale white bread.

Red-fronted Parrakeet (*C. novaezelandiae*) New Zealand

Characteristics: 25 cm (10 in) long. Male—green; brow and front of head red; beak grey-blue; a red patch behind the eyes and on the sides of the rump; bend of wing dark blue; iris red. Female—red patches behind eyes smaller; of less intensive colour; iris orange-red; beak smaller. Young—dull olive green; red only hinted at; paler feet.

Housing and rearing: In the house: Despite its small size, the Red-fronted Parrakeet needs as long a cage as you can manage so that it can get enough exercise. They soon become trusting and learn to repeat words. Being a ground species, it needs only a few perches, but again these must be thick enough for it to walk along.

In the garden: This is an ideal aviary subject, peaceable, trusting and easy to rear. You must have a very large feeding bowl with a high side because this is a species that likes to pick its food up in its feet; it soon tips up small pots or bowls.

The female lays one egg a day, until between five and nine have been laid. They prefer a starling-sized nest box which has been hung up in the shelter. Incubation takes twenty-one days. The female incubates alone and also feeds the young by herself for the first three weeks. Not until four weeks have passed does she cease to remain doggedly in the nest box; then the male takes over the feeding role, and feeds the female, too. It is possible to keep them alongside other species. They are another of the hardier types, which do not need a heated aviary during winter. The young birds pair up quite early on and sometimes lay as early as six months. Older birds that do not continue to breed should be separated and put with another partner, as they will otherwise probably not lay at all.

Yellow-fronted Parrakeet (*C. auriceps*) New Zealand (illustrated p. 44)

Characteristics: 23 cm (9 in) long. Male—green; narrow red brow band; upper head orange; two red patches on each side of the rump; iris dark red; beak lead-coloured. Female—noticeably smaller figure and beak than male; iris orange. Young—dark eyes; head colours duller than adults'.

Housing and rearing. In the house: As for previous type, its voice is even more gentle. Mature birds become extremely tame and give much pleasure through their idiosyncracies.

In the garden: These birds are even more willing to breed than the Red-fronted Parrakeet. Four to nine round white eggs are laid in a starling nest box and incubated by the female for nineteen to twenty-one days. The young leave the nest after about five weeks. The male feeds the female. A successful clutch has been known from birds as young as five months. The Red-fronted and the Yellow-fronted Parrakeets have been known to hybridize.

My female bred in a narrow natural log nestbox which was about 1 m (3 ft 3 in) long. They like narrow old nest sites, and they sometimes gnaw themselves a second way in or out.

Psephotus Parrakeets

Redrump Parrakeet *P. haematonotus*
Manycolour Parrakeet *P. varius*
Paradise Parrakeet *P. pulcherrimus*
Golden-shouldered Parrakeet *P. chrysopterygius* (2 races)
Blue Bonnet *P. haematogaster* (4 races) (*also Northiella*)

The group known as Australian (or Song) Parrakeets come between the true Broadtails and the Grass Parrakeets. They inhabit the dry regions of the savannahs and grasslands. They are not very agile in the trees but their flight is very powerful and tends to follow an undulating pattern. Once the breeding season is over they gather in flocks. There are five species in this genus.

Redrump Parrakeet (*P. haematonotus*)

Characteristics: 28 cm (11 in) long. Male—blue-green; rump red; belly yellow. Female—grey-green; no red on rump. Young—plumage as parents' but duller; beak paler; eyes darker. Young males have only a small amount of red-brown colouring on the rump whilst still in the nestbox. Adult plumage appears in the autumn of the first year.

Origin and habit: Australia: New South Wales, Victoria and eastern South Australia. They are present in great numbers in the dry areas of eastern Australia, to such an extent that the residents no longer notice them. They come into the farms and gardens, and even into the towns. They feed mainly on a wide variety of weeds, and they ignore the wheat fields. However, they can damage gardens. Pairs, which stay together for the whole year, indulge in mutual preening, unusual for Australian Parrakeets. Nest sites are of many different types: hollow trees, embankments, rooftops and old starlings' nests.

General remarks: These are the commonest Parrakeets found in aviaries. They are ideal for beginners. Even experienced breeders should keep a few, though, because they are often used to rear young of another species, most successfully of a related species. One other advantage is the ease with which the sexes are differentiated in the nestbox.

Like Cockatiels, Song Parrakeets are available the whole year round and at a very reasonable price. The voice is a pleasant cooing, hence their name.

Feeding: Canary seed, sunflower, millet, linseed, niger, weeds and chickweed. For breeding: greenfood, germinated seeds and sprouted spray millet.

Housing and rearing. In the house: These Parrakeets are seldom very trusting, and are not suitable as pets.

In the garden: This is another ideal aviary subject that is content with a fairly small aviary. Mine bred twice a year in a 2 m (6 ft 6 in) long flight. They do no damage to wood or wire mesh and you do not need to heat the shelter. They will breed both in the shelter and in the flight and are not fussy about the type of site on offer. Generally speaking, a depth of 40 cm (15¾ in), a width of 23 cm (9 in) and an entrance hole with a diameter of 7 cm (2¾ in) is suitable. Four to seven eggs are laid as early as March or April and incubation lasts nineteen to twenty days. The female does not mind being disturbed during this time. She is fed frequently by the male because she rarely leaves the nest. The young emerge after about four weeks and continue to be fed by her. Since the male chases his young they have to be removed to safety, especially as they often go in for a second brood and no longer want anything to do with their first offspring. They often try to breed in their first year, unsuccessfully.

Mutations: The Yellow Redrump Parrakeet is a popular mutation, but the colour can in no way be described as yellow; it is really a dilute mutation. The mutation was established by an English bird farm in the 1930s.

Manycolour Parrakeet (*P. varius*) (illustrated p. 44)

Characteristics: 30 cm (12 in) long. Male—bluish-green; breast and upper belly green; lower belly and thighs red; rump yellow; brow yellow; crown red; yellow shoulder patch. Female—browny-green with a red shoulder patch; brown-red spots on rear of head. Young—similar to parents but duller; horn-coloured beak. Young males already appear greenish in the nest. Full adult plumage appears around twelve to fourteen months.

Origin and habit: Interior of the whole of Australia, wherever it is arid or scrubby; they merge with the Redrump Parrakeets to the south-east. Now that many woodlands have been cleared, the species has spread further south-west. I saw large numbers of them, and their nest sites, when I was there. When they want to breed, they hound the Budgerigars out of their nests and take them over. They are shy of humans and tend to remain in their bushes or small eucalyptus trees. They search for food almost exclusively on the ground. Analysis of stomach contents has revealed that they eat a variety of grass seeds, berries and fruits, and also insect larvae.

They rear their four to six young in the hollow branches of the eucalyptus trees. As birds of the interior, they adjust the number of offspring according to the rainfall of the year, producing fewer young in the drier years than in the wet ones. They also go in for mutual preening of the plumage.

General remarks: The number of people keeping Manycolour Parrakeets has increased considerably in recent years. What was once an expensive rarity has now become common in aviaries.

The colouring of this species varies greatly, both in the wild and in captivity. It is for this reason that attempts were once made to classify the varieties, and for the same reason that this was abandoned; there are no clear-cut boundaries between the colour variations' habitats. If you want to keep a particular colour of this bird, take a good look at the youngster's parents first to get a definite idea of what its adult colouring will be. Good youngsters already have quite intensive red on the belly. They have pleasant twittering calls.

Feeding: Canary seed, sunflower seed, millet (especially spray millet), oats, apples and carrots, some wild bird food, chickweed. For breeding, add chopped-up hard-boiled egg, spray millet and sprouted oats.

Housing and rearing. In the house: The Manycolour Parrakeet has been reared in an indoor flight. You have to be able to supply freshly-sprouted feed.

In the garden: Specimens bred here can be kept in a flight. They must have a dry, draught-free shelter where they can be kept when it is very cold or wet, and which you can heat a little when necessary. They do not destroy wood or netting and are quieter and calmer than the previous species.

The females begin to be broody quite early on in the year. Unfortunately, as they tend to give up brooding when the chicks are some eight to ten days old, if the weather turns cold the young will die. This is another good reason for putting the nest box inside, where you can supply gentle heat. Once they have settled on one particular nest box they will keep to it for years, so do not alter or move it. A clutch consists of four to six eggs, which need to be incubated for twenty-one days. Two broods a year is not uncommon. The male also helps with the feeding of the young. They leave the nest after almost five weeks and are independent three weeks later.

Paradise Parrakeet (*P. pulcherrimus*)

Characteristics: 28 cm (11 in) long. Male—crown black; nape, back and wings dark brown; brow band, smaller wing coverts, belly, undertail coverts red; head, throat at front and sides and breast blue-green; rump and upper tail greeny-blue. Female—duller colours; yellowish brow band; very little red.

Origin and habit: Australia—northern New South Wales, Queensland. The last confirmed sightings of this species were reported in 1927. Recently, however, reports have been coming in of sightings, and claims to have photographed the bird have been made. The last known records of its breeding in captivity stem from 1880.

Golden-shouldered Parrakeet (*P. chrysopterygius chrysopterygius*)

Characteristics: 25 cm (10 in) long. Male—yellow brow band; smaller black cap; belly, rump, undertail coverts red; wing coverts golden yellow; back brownish; rest of plumage strong blue-green. Female—duller colours; brow band yellow; lower belly red. Young—male has turquoise cheeks, green brow band and dark brown cap. Female has less turquoise on the cheeks, yellowish brow band and similar dark brown cap. Adult plumage appears by the end of the first year.

Origin and habit: Australia—northern Queensland, in the savannahs, feeding on all kinds of grass and weed seeds. It is not very common, and therefore strictly protected.

As used to be the case with the Paradise Parrakeet, its nests are found almost exclusively in termite mounds. It was not until 1922 that they were first found. Young Golden-shouldered Parrakeets live in symbiosis with the caterpillars of one species of moth.

Feeding: Canary seed, millet, weed seeds (unripe where possible), small sunflower kernels, wild bird food, apples, carrots and a soft food or soaked rusk.

Housing and rearing: This Parrakeet, too, is a rarity and therefore expensive. Fortunately, there are now several breeding pairs in captivity and we can only hope that this beautiful and graceful bird will continue to thrive and increase. As the Hooded Parrakeet used to, the Golden-shouldered Parrakeet still prefers to breed in the late autumn or very early in the year, bringing with it the danger of a failed clutch or death of the young because of the cold; particularly since the female soon leaves the nest. Therefore, place the nest box in the shelter where you can heat it if necessary. It has been established that the termites' nests, which are the birds' natural breeding sites, generate a fierce heat, which naturally makes incubation by the parents superfluous. A clutch consists of four to six eggs, incubated for twenty days. The young emerge at four weeks and look just like adult females. However, you can tell the sexes by their heads. The first captive breeding was probably in 1965.

Hooded Parrakeet (*P. chrysopterygius dissimilis*) (illustrated pp. 82 and 93)

Characteristics: 25 cm (10 in) long. Male—black from top of head to eyes; nape black; back dark brown; wings as far as the flights yellow; sides of head and all of underside greenish-yellow; beak dark grey. Female—all upper parts greenish; no yellow in wings; sides of head and underparts pale greenish-blue. Young—young males have a smaller head than young females; no black or yellow. They finally have full adult colouring between fourteen and eighteen months.

Origin and habit: Australia—Northern Territory, where it is still a rarity. Few people inhabit its territory, so not much is known about it. It has been observed on the ground, searching for grass and other seeds. Like its closest relatives, the Golden-shouldered and the Paradise Parrakeets, it too burrows in termite nests to breed. It lays four to six eggs.

Young Hooded Parrakeets.

General remarks: The captive future of this species seems to be assured as there are many good breeding pairs available. They are fussy feeders, preferring to take food from the ground.

Feeding: Canary seed, sunflower, millet (especially spray millet), niger seed, linseed. For breeding, plenty of partially ripe and germinating seeds and fresh weed seeds like orache, persicaria, plantain, and so on. They do not like chopped-up hard-boiled egg.

Housing and rearing. In the garden: You can only keep Hooded Parrakeets in pairs in a flight. They do not destroy wooden structures, so you need have no worries on that score. You must be able to heat the shelter when necessary, because this is another of those species (like the Brown's Rosella) that takes a long time to adjust its breeding cycle to summer. It prefers to breed in autumn or winter, and you must provide temperatures of up to 20°C (68°F). Nowadays, though, they are beginning to show a tendency to breed in any season, so it will not be long before they have adjusted fully to summer.

They nest in normal boxes, laying four to six eggs, which are incubated for twenty days. The young are fledged at four and a half weeks. It is quite common to discover that the parents have abandoned their young. For this reason, many breeders take the eggs or the youngsters away from the nest and put them with a Redrump Parrakeet. However, you cannot do this in winter because the Redrump is already preparing for its own, very early, brood. Of course, the more Redrump pairs you have, the more chances there will be of finding a pair to act as foster parents. The first successful breeding occurred in 1964.

Blue Bonnets (*P.* (also *Northiella*) *haematogaster*)

Yellow-vented Blue Bonnet (*P. haematogaster haematogaster*)

Characteristics: 33 cm (13 in) long. Male—olive-brown upper parts, throat and breast; face, bend of wing, wing edges and coverts blue; dull olive-yellow secondaries; patch of red on belly, rest of under parts yellow. Female—smaller head and beak than male; red patch on belly contains some yellow and is smaller. Young—very similar to adults but with duller colouring. Adult plumage around four to six months, very variable.
Origin and habit: Australia—southern Queensland and northern New South Wales in the dry interior where vegetation is sparse. Their numbers are on the decrease because their habitat—the savannahs—have been turned over to grazing or arable land. They feed on grass and other weeds.
    Yellow-vented Blue Bonnets spend the whole year paired up, though in the non-breeding season they go around in small flocks. You usually find their nests in dead oak trees, not very high up. Some time between August and December they lay four to seven eggs, which the female alone incubates.
General remarks: At present, Yellow-vented Blue Bonnets are less popular than Red-vented Blue Bonnets, despite the fact that a well-coloured specimen of the former is hardly inferior to the latter. You quite often get poorly-coloured Red-vented Blue Bonnets which have very little or no red in their wings. The Little Blue Bonnet is clearly the most costly and sought-after species, although it is no more attractive than a well-coloured Red-vented Blue Bonnet.
    They are very impatient and quarrelsome with other species and must be kept as separate pairs, even outside the breeding season.
    The voice is sometimes pleasantly flute-like, but can also be shrill at times. However, this is not usually troublesome. One of their little peculiarities is that both sexes can raise their head feathers when they are excited. They also enjoy a game, lying on their backs like a kitten at play.
Feeding: Canary seed, sunflower, millet, niger, linseed, salad seedlings and all weeds. It is especially important to give germinated seeds and plenty of chickweed during the breeding season.
Housing and rearing. In the garden: The first successful breeding in Europe took place in 1960. Several years later they were bred in Holland for the first

83

time. Seven eggs were incubated for about twenty-two to twenty-four days and the five young left the nest after four and a half weeks. The male fed the female and she fed the young, as long as they were in the nest. Only one brood per year is expected. The young were in no way shy and looked almost identical to their parents.

The problem would appear to be in selecting compatible birds for pairing, as they are very choosy. You can only keep one settled pair in one flight.

Red-vented Blue Bonnet (*P. haematogaster haematorrhous*)

Characteristics: 32 cm (12½ in) long. Male—wing coverts and rump red; bend of wing turquoise; otherwise colouring as for Yellow-vented. Female—smaller beak and head. Colour is no indication of sex. Young—duller.

Origin and habit: To the east of the previous race, where it is damper, which is why its colouring is more intense. There are still colour variations in the wild, however, and it is said that they hybridize with the Yellow-vented Blue Bonnet where their territories overlap.

General remarks: It is possible to find good breeding pairs in the aviaries of fanciers. As already mentioned, the red colouring is very variable. Birds with a more intensive red are more popular, rarer and more expensive. Sometimes Redrumps are used as foster parents, but this should be reserved only for emergencies, as young reared by their parents are preferable. They can tolerate the climate well, but are not as hardy as the Rosellas. Too much damp, and particularly too much foggy weather, does not suit them at all. As with all the Australian Parrakeets, worming is necessary. They all like to spend much of their time on the ground, so they very easily pick up worms, or worm-eggs.

Feeding: As for Yellow-vented Blue Bonnet.

Breeding: Differs very little from the Yellow-vented. The Red-vented is not nearly so aggressive as the Yellow-vented during the breeding season. A double layer of wire netting is advisable.

Pale Blue Bonnet (*P. haematogaster pallescens* (subspecies)) interior of South Australia (desert type)

Characteristics: Pale underparts and wing coverts; no exact description available.

Little Blue Bonnet (*P. haematogaster narethae*)

Characteristics: 28 cm (11 in) long. Male—turquoise brow; cheeks and upper throat blue; only upper wing coverts red, shading to yellow; bend of wing blue; belly yellowish; rump red; otherwise as Yellow-vented Blue Bonnet.

Female—smaller with less intensive colouring. Young—difficult to sex until first moult.

Origin and habit: Very small territory, confined to the area immediately around the town of Naretha, on the Trans-Continental Railway Line. Continual droughts reduce its breeding zone from year to year. It likes the bush, where trees are scarce. It is extremely shy and usually only seen around the water holes. It flies close to the ground, but likes to perch at the very top of the trees. Its breeding season is from July to December.

General remarks: It was only discovered in the wild in 1921. The first specimens came to Europe towards the end of the 1960s. This species can also be aggressive, particularly towards different species, and double wire netting between neighbouring aviaries is absolutely essential. They are not particularly sensitive to weather, but they do not like damp or fog.

Feeding: As for the other Blue Bonnets. Do not forget to add chickweed, unripe weeds and grated carrot.

Breeding: Three breeders were all successful for the first time in 1971. The birds used a natural log box. Six youngsters were reared from one clutch. Incubation lasts twenty-two days and the young leave the nest after four weeks. If you hope for successful breeding, you need to supply plenty of chickweed, weeds and soft foods.

Grass Parrakeets (*Neophema*)

Turquoise *N. pulchella*
Splendid Parrakeet/Scarlet-chested Parrakeet *N. splendida*
Elegant Parrakeet *N. elegans*
Blue-winged Grass Parrakeet *N. chrysostoma*
Rock Grass Parrakeet *N. petrophila*
Orange-bellied Parrakeet *N. chrysogaster*

This genus comprises six very small but very colourful broadtail Parrakeets which are between 21 and 23 cm (8¼–9 in) in length. They are all very good fliers, but spend much of their time on the ground searching for food. Two species are migrants—they fly to Tasmania to breed and return to the Australian mainland in the winter.

Turquoisine (*N. pulchella*) (illustrated p. 93)

Characteristics: 22 cm (8¾ in) long. Male—green; underside yellow or partially orange; face and small wing coverts blue; red shoulder patch. Female—no red shoulder patch; smaller and duller blue on the head; underparts duller. Young—similar to female, though some young males already have the red shoulder patch, and the underside of the wings is black. Young females have grey underwings and almost always, white spots. Fully coloured between five and seven months.

Origin and habit: Australia—central Queensland and New South Wales. Some seventy years ago the Australians considered the Turquoisine to be almost extinct and it was not until 1920 or thereabouts that it was seen more frequently again. This is particularly puzzling since, only ninety years ago, it was thought to be fairly numerous and its sudden decline cannot be solely attributable to the rapid increase in population in the area. It is presumed that they were the victims of an epidemic. After all, they are seen frequently on the perimeters of towns and housing estates, so they are not afraid of people.

Turquoisines search for their food on the ground. They eat the seeds of grasses, stinging nettles, thistles, chickweed and other wild plants.

They nest in the hollow branches of eucalyptus trees, sometimes only a few metres high, sometimes as much as 20 m (65 ft) up. A clutch consists of four or five eggs.

General remarks: As recently as the beginning of the 1960s, the Turquoisine was still a rarity among breeders. Thanks to its extreme willingness to breed, it soon increased in number and nowadays you will always find it offered for sale at a very low price at any time of the year.

Like all the *Neophema* species, the Turquoisine possesses a very soft, pleasant and melodious voice, so that it is difficult to imagine that they belong to the parrot family at all. After World War II, all Turquoisines in Europe had yellow underparts, but now you often see them with orange patches of one size or another. This is not a result of hybridizing, however.

Feeding: Canary seed, millet, niger seed, linseed, some hemp and small sunflower seeds. Some birds also like figs. In addition, diced carrots and apples, chickweed and other weed seeds are taken. For breeding, plenty of sprouting millet sprays, chopped-up hard-boiled egg and chickweed.

Housing and rearing. In the house: Hand-reared Turquoisines, especially males, grow very tame and can be kept in a cage, as long as they have some free-flying time every day. They have been known to become so tame that they follow their owners around like a dog.

Successful breedings have been reported from birds which were kept in bird rooms or large cages measuring 1 m (3 ft 3 in) in length by 60 cm (2 ft) wide. It is best to place the cage at eye-level so that the birds can feel less disturbed and more secure.

In the garden: A flight with an unheated shelter is ideal. An external length of about 2 m (6 ft 6 in) is enough. Like all the Grass Parrakeets, it does not destroy wood, though it does enjoy gnawing at fresh green twigs when they are offered. Those birds which have been bred here for generations are very hardy and can endure even the most adverse of weather conditions. One of mine stayed out all night a few years ago when the temperature was −16°C

(3°F) and there was ice and snow everywhere. Next morning he was as bright and cheerful as ever and went on to breed successfully early the next year.

Keep your breeding pair separately as they can be rather aggressive towards other birds. Do not keep a related species in the adjoining aviary.

The female lays her eggs, from four to seven, in April and sits for twenty days. Some three weeks after leaving the nest, the young are independent. You then have to take them away from their parents, which start another brood and the father begins to hound his offspring unmercifully. Only allow a third brood from your more mature specimens. They do not object to being observed on the nest. You can even take the eggs from under the female if you need to. They are mature at one year; sometimes a female will lay as early as six months, but the eggs are infertile.

Mutations: A yellow mutation has been established. The birds are canary yellow and retain the red shoulder patch.

Splendid Parrakeet (*N. splendida*) (illustrated p. 94)

Characteristics: 21 cm (8¼ in) long. Male—upper parts green; blue head; throat and upper breast red; lower parts yellow; wing coverts pale blue. Female—olive green upper parts; head pale blue; throat and breast greenish; remaining underparts yellow. (This is very similar to the female Turquoisine but here the light blue of the head and wings is very much paler.) Young—as female but duller. You can distinguish a young male when the red breast feathers begin to appear. When they are a little older, the underwing feathers of a female are greyish, whereas a male's are black. Moulting takes place at varying times, but usually between three and five months. On occasion, a young male may leave the nest when he has a few red breast feathers.

Origin and habit: Australia—inland areas of western New South Wales across to Western Australia. At one time, the population of Splendid Parrakeets was threatened. It has become rare in eastern Australia, while its numbers in the west have recovered. Its prefers desert-like regions where the bush is sparse and the grasses are plentiful. It stays in one chosen area and is not shy of people.

As a resident of dry areas, the Splendid Parrakeet has very little need for drinking water. It is said to stay away from drinking pools for several days on end. It feeds on the ground off a variety of grass seeds, especially the spinifex.

Like its relatives, it too breeds in hollow branches of low trees and bushes, mostly acacias. After the breeding season they go around in small flocks. Splendid Parrakeets enjoy strict protection.

General remarks: No fancier can fail to be impressed by its magnificent colouring, for it is the most beautiful of the whole genus.

At first, many would-be breeders suffered disappointments with this bird, which was an expensive rarity. As an inhabitant of the desert regions, it did not take to our damper climate and many died. Acclimatization was a slow process and only gradually did a hardy strain develop. Nowadays, we are lucky enough to be able to buy hardy specimens whenever we wish at a very reasonable price. Wherever possible, you should winter them in a frost-free dry room, especially the young birds that have not finished moulting. The most beautiful males have a particularly large red area on the breast which should come to a definite end, not shade into the next colour. Since this red patch is not fully visible on the young male, you can only go by the appearance of its male parent when deciding how good it is likely to be. Its voice is a delicate chirruping, more like that of a finch.

Feeding: Canary seed, millet, particularly spray millet, with niger, maw, linseed, salads and a little hemp, chopped-up carrots and apples, plenty of chickweed and germinating weed seeds. For breeding, additional sprouting spray millet or other germinating seeds and chopped-up egg should be fed (but not too much oily seed as many birds are inclined to become fat).

Housing and rearing. In the house: It is possible to rear Splendid Parrakeets in a cage as long as it is not less than 1 m (3 ft 3 in) long. Bird rooms or lofts are much better as they give the birds plenty of space for flying exercise, which is important as their somewhat phlegmatic natures can allow them to become overweight. For cage rearing, then, plenty of greenfood, apples and carrots are important. These birds are not shy, and soon get used to their owner, sometimes feeding from his hand. As you would expect, therefore, hand-reared birds become very tame. They, too, must have a large cage and plenty of exercise.

In the garden: You must have an aviary which is at least 2 m (6 ft 6 in) long for Splendid Parrakeets. It is vital that the shelter is dry and draughtproof. When it is very frosty, foggy or damp you need to be able to heat the shelter a little. A hygrometer (to measure humidity) is invaluable. The birds feel better according to how dry it is. (They are a desert species, remember!)

You need starling nest boxes for breeding. The birds do not mind if they are square or round and mine have bred both in the shelter and in the flight. However, make sure that no rain can get into the box.

Both in the wild and in captivity, it has been observed that the female uses her rump feathers to carry small bits of leaves and grass stalks into the nest, just like the Lovebirds do, probably to provide moisture for the eggs.

As a rule, they lay five or six eggs which need incubating for about nineteen days. There is no need to separate the young from their parents in a hurry—when mine had a second brood, the males were perfectly tolerant and friendly towards their firstborn. Moulting is, for young Splendid Parrakeets, a somewhat critical phase. If you want to determine sex early on, pull a few breast feathers out. If they grow back red, you know the bird is a male.

Splendid Parrakeets have reared five young when they were only eight months old. It is quite possible to house them with finches.

Mutations: A blue mutation has been established. The most beautiful specimens have a blue upper side and are white underneath.

Elegant Parrakeet (*N. elegans*)

Characteristics: 23 cm (9 in) long. Male—olive green; underparts yellow or greenish-yellow with reddish patch on belly; dark blue brow band edged in pale blue; underwing coverts blackish. Female—underparts greener; brow band narrower with pale blue edging very narrow; underwing coverts grey-black; only very rarely is there a red belly patch; head smaller and narrower than male's. Young—greener; brow band barely noticeable; not always possible to tell a young male; often have wider pale blue edging to brow band; underwing coverts darker. Flights of female young are pale grey, of young male are dark grey. Adult colouring between six and eight months.
Origin and habit: Australia—southern Queensland across to New South Wales, Victoria and South Australia to central Western Australia. Elegant Parrakeets are very common and continually on the increase. Such spontaneous increase is a direct result of the forest clearances, since this is a species which avoids dense woodlands.

Its food is seeds of grasses, weeds and other wild plants. Splendid Parrakeets feed on the seeds which they take from the clover and wheat fields. I saw them doing this when I was in Western Australia, although they are very difficult to spot because their colouring is excellent camouflage.

Their call is a gentle 'sit' and their song a twittering chatter, but only by the males. Outside the breeding season, they fly around in small flocks; during breeding they generally stay in pairs. You find their nests in hollow tree trunks or branches, and also in decaying tree stumps. I once saw a nest in a eucalyptus tree about 10 m (33 ft) up, but it only measured 12 cm (4¾ in) across at the most.
General remarks: During the past twenty years or so captive breeding has increased the popularity of this beautiful bird enormously. Now, you can buy Elegants at any time of the year and, as a result, the prices have naturally dropped quite rapidly. Bearing in mind its very wide distribution area in the wild, it is not surprising that colour variations are common. The most popular are the olive-green ones with strong yellow colouring on their underparts and a bright orange patch on the belly. You also get quite plain ones, just greenish, which are not nearly so popular. A really strongly coloured Elegant Parrakeet is a very beautiful and graceful bird.
Feeding: Canary seed, sunflower, oats, millet (especially spray millet), niger seed, linseed and some hemp; small diced carrots or apples, and chickweed. For breeding, feed millet seedlings or sunflower shoots, some chopped-up hard-boiled egg and partially ripe weed seeds.
Housing and rearing. In the house: There are no problems associated with

breeding in a bird room, a loft or in a room of your house where the birds fly free. One of my acquaintances reared them successfully in a 2 m (6 ft 6 in) long flight in his loft, where very large windows ensured adequate light. Only a hand-reared bird that was taken from the nest early on should be kept as a pet.

In the garden: Elegant Parrakeets are ideal for the aviary since, like the other Grass Parrakeets, they do not destroy wood and are hardy in all weathers. Of course, you still need shelter for them, though it is not necessary to heat it.

They prefer to breed in the shelter, rather than in the open. They take to a starling nest box immediately, preferably one with an entrance hole measuring 6 cm (2¼ in) across and an overall diameter of 18 cm (7 in) at the base. As early as the end of March or the beginning of April the female lays four to seven eggs, which she alone incubates. They hatch after about nineteen days and the young birds leave the nest after four weeks. They are fed mainly by the male because the female starts to brood again soon after. I have never seen the parents attack their young, as the Turquoisine does, so I always leave my young with their parents for months. If you do this, in order to distinguish the old female, you must ring all the offspring.

Elegants have been known to breed as early as eight months of age, but if they do not do this spontaneously, leave them until they are about ten or twelve months old, as eggs laid by younger birds are usually infertile.

Blue-winged Grass Parrakeet (*N. chrysostoma*) (illustrated p. 93)

Characteristics: 23.5 cm (9½ in) long. Male—green; brow band as far as the eyes blue with very pale blue edges; wing coverts deep blue; primaries black; throat and upper breast greenish-yellow; belly yellowish, sometimes with an orange spot. Female—narrower brow band; smaller head and body; lower body duller colours and without orange spot (but not always); primaries grey-black. Young—brow band barely visible; duller colours; less blue in the wings. Adult plumage around eight to ten months. It can be difficult to sex the young, though you can sometimes go by the shape of the head, size, colour and primaries with a certain amount of assurance.

Origin and habit: Australia—New South Wales, Victoria, South Australia and Tasmania. You will find the Blue-winged Grass Parrakeet in both woodland and meadows, in damp as well as cultivated regions. Because it is so adaptable, its numbers are continually on the increase. In Tasmania and the coastal regions of South Australia it is a summer visitor, migrating north for the winter. However, some specimens have been known to winter in Tasmania.

It seeks its food on the ground where it is practically invisible, due to its excellent camouflage. It feeds on grass seed, wild berries and weed seeds, and can be seen in the orchards or wheat fields, looking for food.

This is one of the Grass Parrakeets that lives colonially. They even go around in large flocks during the breeding season and seem to get along without quarrelling. Their nests are frequently very close to one another, and sometimes in the same tree. It is the female who chooses the site. She lays four to six eggs.

General remarks: Only fairly recently has the Blue-wing come back on to the European market. They have not achieved great popularity, probably because their colouring is not dramatic and their temperament is rather phlegmatic. As a consequence of this apathy, they tend to become overweight.

Feeding: Sunflower seeds, canary seed, millet, oats, chopped-up carrots and apples, chickweed. In addition, some niger, linseed and a little hemp. Restrict the quantity of oily seed! Occasionally, they may take to rowan berries.

Housing and rearing: The Blue-winged Grass Parrakeet must have a flight measuring at least 3 m (9 ft 9 in) long so that it can get enough exercise and keep its weight down. It should not be caged as it is very lethargic.

In the garden: They do well in a long flight. Like their relatives, they do not chew wood. Birds bred here do not need winter heat, but do not forget to provide a shelter. If you have a large aviary, you can happily keep two pairs of this species together. Apart from a few harmless tiffs, they are quite peaceable. This behaviour is born out by the way they live in the wild—nesting close together.

Rock Grass Parrakeet (*N. petrophila*)

Characteristics: 21 cm (8¼ in) long. Male—green; brow band blue; pale blue edging; belly and rump greeny-yellow, sometimes with belly patch (orange); pale blue lores and around the eyes; wings black with bluish tinge to the outer feathers. Female—same colouring, less blue on the brow and smaller size. Young—duller colouring; brow band barely visible.

Origin and habit: Australia—coastal regions of south and south-west Australia. The Rock Grass Parrakeet is only found on the narrow islands and adjoining coasts, where it keeps to the sandy and rocky areas. It is a very rapid mover on the ground, only taking to the air when it is absolutely necessary. This may have something to do with the windy conditions which prevail.

It feeds on weed seeds and a particularly succulent plant which is local and plentiful.

There are no trees as such in its habitat, so it breeds in stony hollows or chalk cliffs. Where the spot is particularly favourable, they nest very close to one another, just like the Blue-wings. The natural breeding season falls in September to November. It is said to be common for them to have two broods a year.

General remarks: This species is still a rarity to many breeders, and only a very few pairs exist in Europe. Because of its fairly unimpressive plumage, it is not expected that many breeders will take to it. They have been reared in a normal nestbox, but humidity is of prime importance.

Orange-bellied Parrakeet (*N. chrysogaster*)

Characteristics: 22 cm (8¾ in) long. Male—brow band blue; lores, head, breast and undertail coverts yellowy-green; back and rump grass-green; centre of belly orange. Female—duller colours; narrower brow band; less widespread orange area on the underside. Young—not fully coloured until eight or nine months old, difficult to sex until then.

Origin and habit: Australia—coastal regions of South Australia, Victoria, New South Wales and the islands of Tasmania. It is now a rarity almost everywhere, only appearing with regularity, it seems, on the small islands between Tasmania and the mainland. It inhabits the bushy areas near the coast, which are very wet in parts. Grass seeds are its main food. It is said to nest almost on the ground, laying four or five eggs some time between November and January.

General remarks: This small Grass Parrakeet is very closely related to the Blue-wing. The former's yellow-green lore-stripe is of the utmost importance in distinguishing it. Only a very few have ever been imported into Europe, though I am sure that many fanciers would welcome it if it could be

Page 93
Top left: Hooded Parrakeet (*Psephotus chrysopterygius dissimilis*)
Top right: Turquoisine (*Neophema pulchella*)
Bottom left: Blue-winged Grass Parrakeet (*Neophema chrysostoma*)
Bottom right: Bourke's Parrakeet (*Neophema bourkii*)

Page 94
Top left: Splendid or Scarlet-chested Parrakeet (*Neophema splendida*)
Top right: Swainson's/Blue Mountain Lorikeet (*Trichoglossus haematodus moluccanus*)
Bottom left: Ornate Lorikeet (*Trichoglossus ornatus*)
Bottom right: Black-capped Lory (*Domicella lory*)

Page 95
Top: Abyssinian Lovebird (*Agapornis taranta*)
Bottom left: Red-faced Lovebird (*Agapornis pullaria*)
Bottom right: Peach-faced Lovebird (*Agapornis roseicollis*)

Page 96
Top left: Fischer's Lovebird (*Agapornis personata fischeri*)
Top right: Masked Lovebird (*Agapornis personata personata*)
Bottom left: Nyasa Lovebird (*Agapornis personata lilianae*)
Bottom right: Black-cheeked Lovebird (*Agapornis personata nigrigensis*)

imported or reared in greater quantities. Even in Australia, so I am told, not many people breed it, and those that do guard it like a precious jewel. There are several in Holland and Belgium. Youngsters—two in number—were first reared in Europe in 1971.

Bourke's Parrakeets (*Neopsephotus*, also *Neophema*)

Bourke's Parrakeet (*N. bourkii*) (illustrated p. 93)

Characteristics: 22 cm (8¾ in) long. Male—upper parts brownish; under parts pink to red; pale blue flanks, brow and eyebrow stripes; whitish patch beneath the eyes. Front of cheeks also whitish. Female—paler colours; *no* blue brow band. Young—as female but even duller colours. Full adult colours at seven to nine months. Sometimes you can tell a male quite early on by the few blue brow feathers which appear.

Origin and habit: Western Australia, central Australia and New South Wales. Its distribution range cannot be defined precisely because the migration pattern varies. For many years, people thought that it was extinct but in recent years more and more have been seen. Some ornithologists felt that the distribution of this species was in some way tied to the distribution of sheep farms. The sheep roam the plains in their millions, eating the seeds and trampling the grasses underfoot, so little is left for the Bourke's Parrakeet to feed on. As a result, its numbers were decimated. When, as a result of a year-long drought, a vast number of sheep died, the numbers of Bourke's Parrakeets rose dramatically. They spend much time on the ground, searching for food. They can run quickly and are hard to spot because of their camouflage colouring. Nests are built as high as 3 m (9 ft 9 in) up a tree, in hollow branches.

General remarks: Formerly, Bourke's Parrakeet was classed with the *Neophema*. For a long time its name was spelt incorrectly—it is called after a former governor, Sir R. Bourke.

People keep Bourke's Parrakeets because they have so many good points. They are undemanding, peaceable, quiet, quick to grow tame, easy to breed and always reasonably priced. All these qualities make up for its lack of bright colours. Bourke's Parrakeets are at their most lively early in the morning and at dusk.

Feeding: Canary seed, white millet, maw, niger, linseed, small sunflower seeds and diced carrot. Some, though not all, enjoy chickweed. For breeding, feed chopped-up hard-boiled egg, biscuits, spray millet, soaked white bread and unripe grass seeds.

Housing and rearing. In the house: Bourke's Parrakeet is a good house bird, whether kept as a single specimen, with birds of a different type or for breeding. They do not chew wood and young birds quickly become tame and can be let out to fly around the room.

If you want them to breed, put a pair into a cage not less than 80 cm (2 ft 8 in) tall. They readily take to a starling nestbox or a Budgie nestbox once they are more than one year old. The female incubates her four or five eggs (sometimes more) for eighteen days. The young leave the nest after four weeks and at first are fairly wild, though this does not last long. Two broods are normal, but never allow more in one year. Bourke's are good foster parents and can be used to rear others of their genus (such as Turquoisine and Splendid Parrakeets), and Many-colour Parrakeets, amongst others. Some breeders pluck a few brow feathers from the young just as they have left the nest, so that they can encourage the growth of new feathers, which will help them to sex the birds.

In the garden: This species is well suited to the aviary. Take care, however, to protect them from more than a few degrees of frost because they cannot tolerate it. The shelter must be absolutely dry and draught-free. As a bird of the dry steppes, Bourke's does not take kindly to European damp and foggy weather.

It is usually possible to keep these in with Budgerigars and Cockatiels, despite the occasional little quarrels which may arise. More males than females are offered for sale.

Mutations: Isabelle and yellow mutations are sometimes reared, both with dark red eyes. They are similar to each other, but the Isabelles are genetically recessive and the yellow ones are sex-linked.

Swift Parrakeet (*Lathamus*)

Swift Parrakeet (*L. discolor*)

Characteristics: 24 cm (9½ in) long. Male—upper parts green; underparts yellowish; brow, throat and underwings red; the red on the throat has a bright red edge; undertail coverts sprinkled with red. Female—only slightly less colourful than the male with smaller red throat and brow patches. Young— all colours duller no red speckles on undertail. Easier to tell the sexes whilst still in the nest, as female is smaller and narrower in the head, and brow is only faint red. Adult plumage appears at around six months.

Origin and habit: Tasmania; probably only a winter visitor to Victoria, New South Wales and southern parts of Queensland. It is quite common on Tasmania, where it is found high up in the trees, in the thickest foliage, as well as in parks, gardens and even built-up areas. Numbers vary in the different areas as the birds tend to follow the blossoms from tree to tree, and thus pursue a somewhat nomadic existence.

They are generally found amongst the blossoms of the eucalyptus trees, feeding on the nectar. They also eat berries, small seeds and insects. Their breeding season falls during our winter. Two to four eggs are laid.

General remarks: Formerly it was believed that this species was related to the Lories, but current practice is to class it with the Broadtails, for a variety of reasons. It exhibits characteristics that belong to both groups.

Nowadays, many people who formerly spent their time dreaming of owning a Swift Parrakeet, do own one. They are popular because of their calm, gentle and peace-loving temperaments.

Feeding: Sunflower, spray millet, oats and groats, carrots, apples, orange segments, dry or soaked rusks, chickweed, berries and other sweet fruits and dried insects. For breeding, feed plenty of ripe fruits, extra seedlings, chopped-up hard-boiled egg and soaked white bread. They also love runny sweet foods, such as honey or babyfood.

Housing and rearing. In the house: Your best chances of a breeding success are in a bird room or indoor aviary, but this should be at least 3 m long and 2 m high (9 ft 9 in × 6 ft 6 in). Wood is suitable as they do not destroy it. They lay three or four eggs and the young leave the nest after five weeks. My birds ejected all the nesting material I provided—peat, sawdust, and so on—so the nest should have a concave base.

In the garden: Swift Parrakeets that have been bred here can be kept out of doors, but they must have shelter during the winter.

Budgerigar (*Melopsittacus*)

Budgerigar (*M. undulatus*) (illustrated p. 100)

Characteristics: 18 cm (7 in) long. Male—blue cere (skin around nostrils); iris yellow. Female—brownish cere; iris yellow. Young—duller colours; small and irregular spots on throat; cere flesh coloured, bluish-white or mauve. Young females in the nest have a white border to the nostrils, young males do not; iris of both sexes is black. Plumage begins to take on adult colours around three months, and is completed by six to eight months.

Origin and habit: Australian interior. The wild Budgerigar is green with a yellow head and wavy black and yellow pattern to the back feathers. Colour mutations are rare. It is the commonest of the Australian Parrakeets. It is found everywhere, except in very dense woodland and on the island of Tasmania, and it does inhabit very dry areas of coastland.

During long droughts, the birds migrate in huge flocks and often turn up in areas that they would otherwise never frequent. Even though it has adapted very well to surviving very dry periods, it still leads a nomadic existence. As soon as it arrives in an area where it has recently rained, it begins to breed. If it rains a second time, it breeds a second time; if not, it

A variety of Budgerigars.

continues its migration, thus, it always makes best use of whatever food and habitat are available. Freshly sprouted seeds are necessary to rear the young and these are most plentiful soon after a fall of rain. So, breeding is more dependent on rainfall than on seasons.

Budgerigars are very active all day long during a rainy period, whereas during a drought they only become active in the mornings and evenings. This is all to do with the water holes; they often gather in their hundreds of thousands at the few water holes. They love to perch in the giant eucalyptus trees that line the river banks. It is here that they nest, several pairs to a tree, in groups of twenty to forty birds.

Budgerigars use the smallest possible holes by which to enter their nests, presumably so that larger Parrakeets cannot get in after them. In particular, Manycolour Parrakeets do not tolerate Budgerigars and often drive them away. After one particularly heavy rainstorm, one Budgerigar nest full of youngsters was found to be 30 cm (12 in) lower in the tree trunk; the young were quite chirpy. The rain had driven the nest mass further and further down the tree trunk, but the nest material had let the water drain through, so the young birds had not drowned.

A typical clutch contains three to five eggs. In good weather conditions, several broods are reared in succession, often by birds that are themselves only three or four months old.

General remarks: It was John Gould who first made the existence of the Budgerigar known when he brought some to England in 1840. Over the years, massive imports of the birds made them very widely known. In 1879 some 80,000 pairs were imported into England and by 1894 the Australian Government had put a total embargo on their export. Many birds died during the very long voyage, sometimes due to poor travelling conditions. At first prices were high, but they gradually dropped as the numbers of home-bred birds increased.

The first yellow mutations were reported in 1872 in Belgium, where Lutinos occurred as well. It was also in Belgium that the first blues appeared (1878), and the first Dark Greens occurred in 1920; these led to Olives. In the early 1920s, Cobalt, White Blue and Mauve specimens were bred. Later many more colour mutations arose and have led to ever more variations to this day. Budgerigars can live up to eighteen years.

Feeding: Canary seed, millets (especially spray and white), oats and groats, chickweed and apples.

Housing and rearing. In the house: If possible, use a cage which has horizontal bars so that the bird will find climbing easier; avoid putting too many toys in the cage because this restricts its freedom of movement. It is much better to provide a 'playground' on the top of the cage; after all, the bird has to be let out for exercise at least once a day. You will find it easy to lure a recalcitrant bird back into the cage with a piece of millet.

If you hope to have a thoroughly tame bird one day, start with a youngster just out of the nest or a hand-reared male, if possible. As mentioned above, in 'characteristics', young can only be sexed by the cere colour.

Females can also become very tame, but you have a better chance with a male. It is certainly only the males who make good talkers. The talent for mimicry is vastly different from bird to bird; one will learn a large number of sounds and learn them quickly, another will only ever manage a very few words. Teach a few words at a time, very gradually, and speak very clearly. Try to link the words to a particular action or event. Once these are known, add a few new ones but do not forget to repeat the old ones. Naturally, you will only succeed with a bird that is well tamed and not afraid of people or of sitting on your hand. Do not let your Budgerigar fly loose round the room at first—the chase to recapture it will only make it afraid. Give it time to get used to its cage and the room around it. Get it used to your hand by tickling it through the bars, then try this through the open door. Feed it dainties, such as apple and biscuits, as you try to tempt it on to your finger. Only when it is really happy about being with human beings can you let it out for a free flight.

At first, only let it out at night, when the lights are on. The birds are generally calmer and more relaxed by night. If it will not go back into its cage voluntarily, put the light out when you have it on your finger. Then you can pop it in without having to chase it round the room. One advantage of doing it this way is that the bird is not aware of the hand which is coming to catch it. If you stick to these rules, you will experience endless pleasure from its antics.

Budgies are the easiest species to breed. Before you buy any birds, decide if you are aiming to breed a specific colour and buy accordingly.

It is quite all right to begin breeding from them once they are over nine months old. As a rule, they will provide good offspring for about five years, as long as you do not overbreed them. Once older than this, they tend to be less fruitful and the young are weaker. One good indicator of breeding condition is the waxy cere; if it is smooth, the birds are young and fertile, if it is rough and uneven, it is probably an older bird and breeding will be less profitable.

They breed at any time of the year. If this should happen to be during the winter, you must increase the amount of light by keeping the lights on so that the young are given enough food by their parents. If you are aiming to breed for showing, you are practically compelled to breed in the winter so that your birds will have finished moulting by the following autumn and be ready for the shows. Do not allow more than three broods a year. To achieve this, separate the sexes out of the breeding season. Then they will be all the readier to breed again next time.

One pair will breed in a fairly small cage, two in a cage which is at least 1 m (3 ft 3 in) long. If you are breeding for exhibition you have to keep them as isolated pairs in order to be certain of the parentage of the young. The one advantage of keeping large numbers together is that they choose their own partner very readily and so breed more quickly. On no account put more females than males together for breeding; always aim to have the numbers even. You need two nest boxes per pair to avoid arguments. Put them at the same height but as far apart as possible.

The number of eggs in a clutch varies. Usually, you can expect five or six, but sometimes you might get as many as ten. After laying the second egg, the female sits tight and the eggs start to hatch after a further seventeen days. The males visit the female on the nest now and then. The young open their eyes at eight to ten days of age and leave the nest at five weeks. Some fourteen days later, put the young birds in a separate cage.

It is possible to house Budgerigars with Cockatiels, including during breeding. Male Budgerigars live quite peacefully with other species but females quarrel and fight. Their very lively behaviour can also hinder another species from breeding.

In the garden: Budgerigars are hardy birds and live in an aviary very contentedly. As usual, provide a shelter, but on no account heat it. You only need gentle heat for breeding. A breeding pair generally need about 2 cu m (6½ cu ft) of space. You can keep young or non-breeders here in greater numbers, of course.

Since Budgies are very good fliers, plenty of flying room is essential. A long flight which has branches or perches across the corners only, is ideal. They like to paddle in sand or damp grass. Do not forget to provide a space for the youngsters which have achieved independence.

Free flight: Since the wild Budgerigar is a nomad of the steppes and bush, it does not feel tied to any one particular place. Only the youngsters feel like this, and then only temporarily. That is why they will fly off at the first opportunity, no matter how tame they have become. You can only allow them the freedom of your garden whilst they feel tied to the nest by their young. Once these have begun to fly, however, the parents will begin to wander.

Mutations: Sometimes Budgerigars make good foster mothers. For example, they have reared a Cockatiel until it reached the age of six weeks. After that, the breeder had to take over. They have also been known to foster Turquoisines, Peach-faced Lovebirds (*Agapornis roseicollis*) and Fischer's Lovebird (*A. personata fischeri*).

Red Lories (*Eos*), Wedgetailed Lories (*Trichoglossus*), Broadtailed Lories (*Domicella*)

Eos Lories

Violet-necked Lory *E. squamata* (5 races)
Red Lory/Moluccan Lory *E. bornea* (4 races)

Trichoglossus Lorikeets

Rainbow Lory *T. haematodus* (22 races)
Ornate Lory *T. ornatus*

Domicella Lories

Black-capped/Tri-coloured Lory *D. lory* (8 races)
Purple-capped Lory *D. domicella*
Chattering Lory *D. garrula* (2 races)

Origin and habit: Philippines, East Indies, the Moluccas, New Guinea and its surrounding islands and certain areas of Polynesia and Australia. Brightly-coloured Lories are woodland birds which inhabit the same territory as Cockatoos. They are skilful climbers and many types are fast fliers.

Lories feed on the nectar and pollen of blossoms, fruits and berries and occasionally on insects. They can do this easily because of the peculiar structure of their tongue—it ends in several 'fronds', rather like the bristles of a brush. They nest in hollows, and most species lay only two eggs.

General remarks: Certain *Trichoglossus* Lories are frequently imported. Among these, therefore, it is no surprise to find some which are very nervous or excited and which try to flee from any human approach.

It is easy to rear young Lories on watery babyfood.

By contrast, *Domicella* and *Eos* Lories are imported in small numbers or pairs. Naturally, their prices are higher, especially if they are hand-tamed birds. The natives particularly like to take young Lories from their nests to rear as house pets. One way of telling such specimens is by the ring of bone or leather which is fastened round a leg, to which a chain could be fixed.

Tame Lories, in contrast to Macaws, African Greys and some of the Amazons, are very friendly towards everybody. They do not have particular favourites. They are very playful and amusing. They will perform somersaults, lie down on their backs, and make a grab at anything and everything which comes within their reach.

Their drawback is the somewhat difficult nature of their foodstuffs and the liquid droppings. No lory can exist on seed for any length of time.

Feeding: It is not difficult to make up fresh daily a liquid mixture containing such items as baby cereal, condensed milk, honey or glucose and malt extract. Nowadays, though, you can get a powdered food (meant for babies) which contains fruit with honey and vitamins (all dried) which is a very good and nourishing substitute. You only need to stir in some liquid. In addition, feed sweet fruits, all types of berries, biscuit, soaked white bread, chopped-up carrots and boiled rice.

As supplements try sprouting sunflower, rye or oats (mixed with the rice, perhaps). When they get used to it, offer the seed before it sprouts (especially to *Trichoglossus* species). It is always best to offer all foods at about head height as Lories do not really like feeding off the ground.

Housing and rearing. In the house: As already touched upon, you need to be able to cope with the virtually liquid excreta which Lories produce. Since they like to hang from the bars of their cages, they are also likely to foul the floor of the room. A box-cage, which has an easily-cleaned interior, is of great value provided that it is large enough for these very active birds. Glass plates must be easy and quick to remove and clean (have two of every item).

One ideal place to keep these birds indoors is the attic. Or you can furnish your loft or any other room specially to take Lories.

A tamed individual or pair is best for keeping in the house, since many types have a very loud voice. They are not very ready talkers, *Trichoglossus* species even less than *Domicellas*. The latter grow tame more quickly, be they males or females.

In the garden: Lories are well able to tolerate a few degrees of frost, provided that they have a nest box in which to roost. During a severe frost their feet suffer first. Thus, it is always best to have a good stout nest box in the shelter for them to retreat to in very cold weather.

Trichoglossus Lorikeets are very fast fliers and for this reason need a flight which measures at least 3 m (9 ft 9 in) in length; however, if the flight is too long, it will have the effect of making the birds very shy. Some types have bred quite often, others very little. The problem lies in determining sexes. In captivity, no more than two eggs are laid. There does not appear to be one specific breeding time and you may even get three or four broods in one year if you own a good breeding pair. A prerequisite for this is good feeding.

Red Lories

Violet-necked Lory (*E. squamata*) the Moluccas, Halmahera and neighbouring islands

Characteristics: 25 cm (9¾ in) long. Male—red with a bluish nape and throat band; centre of belly violet; flights brown; beak red.

Breeding has often been successful; in 1927 the first success occurred in Europe. The male's display is a kind of dance round the female. They always lay two eggs. The young leave the nest after a good two months and are fed by their parents for a further two weeks. The female does not usually object to nest inspection whilst incubating.

Red Lory/Moluccan Lory (*E. bornea*) Ambon, Ceram and the Moluccas

Characteristics: 30 cm (12 in) long. Male and female—red; shoulder and undertail coverts blue; beak orange.

This Lory is often offered for sale and has been bred on many occasions. One German success was by Mr Banzhaff in Gestetten who reared two youngsters in 1976. Red Lories grow very tame and can be very affectionate.

Trichoglossus Lorikeets

Rainbow Lorikeet (*T. haematodus*) Molucca, Ceram, Ambon, Flores, Sumba, Bali, Lombok, New Guinea and eastern Australia

Swainson's/Blue Mountain Lorikeet (*T. haematodus moluccanus*) eastern Australia (illustrated p. 94)

Characteristics: 33 cm (13 in) long. Male—green; head and centre of belly blue; breast yellow-orange; yellow-green nape band; beak and iris red. Female—iris orange; breast colouring often less intensive than male's. Young—as adult but smaller (especially the tail feathers); beak not pure red.

The Swainson's or Blue Mountain Lorikeet is the one most frequently kept by breeders. The main reasons for this are not just its magnificent colouring, but also the ease with which it breeds and its hardiness in all types of weather. However, they are becoming rare, and quite frequently the name is used for other subspecies of *haematodus*.

They quickly get used to eating sunflower, oats, canary seed, and so on, but they still need nectar daily, plus apples and carrots quite often, and the occasional grape.

They are best kept as pairs. The male's display consists of a weaving swaying motion, during which you might hear a curious rustling sound. Females only lay two eggs, which they incubate for twenty-five days. Both parents feed the youngsters. They leave the nest after seven or eight weeks, complete with plumage like that of their parents. It is possible to get two or three broods a year, which are not linked to any specific season.

They are not fussy about where they breed, using any box which would suit a starling or woodpecker, with an entrance hole about 8 cm (3 in) across. Put several centimetres of woodshavings or peat at the bottom. Since Lorikeets also roost in the nest box, it needs cleaning out occasionally. Mine chose a natural log nestbox which was about 50 cm (1 ft 8 in) deep.

Forsten's Lorikeet (*T. haematodus forsteni*) Sumbawa

Characteristics: 27 cm (10½ in) long. Male and female—green; head, throat and belly dark blue; sides of belly yellow; neck band greenish-yellow; breast bright red and beak reddish.

Many successful breedings have been recorded.

Mitchell's/Red-breasted Lorikeet (*T. haematodus mitchellii*) Islands of Bali and Lombok

Characteristics: 24 cm (9½ in) long. Male—green; head purplish-brown to dark violet; red breast; blackish-purple belly with greenish sides; beak orange. Female—smaller than male, with a flatter head shape.

This small Lorikeet is occasionally offered for sale or bred. It is very lively and easily excited.

Ornate Lorikeet (*T. ornatus*) Sulawesi and neighbouring islands (illustrated p. 94)

Characteristics: 23 cm (9 in) long. Male and female—green; upper head dark blue with a yellow patch behind the ears; throat, breast and cheeks red; blackish diagonal markings across a red breast; yellow sides; belly and nape green with yellow wavy edgings.

The Ornate Lorikeet has exceptionally brilliant plumage. It is a lively and impetuous bird with a strong voice which can frequently be heard. Hand-reared specimens can be very affectionate and tame.

This species is not difficult to breed, and is not regularly imported.

Domicella Lories

Black-capped/Tri-coloured Lory (*D. lory*) New Guinea (illustrated p. 94)

Characteristics: 30 cm (12 in) long. Male—black cape; sides of head red, also throat, nape band, sides of body and underwing coverts; remaining underparts, breast band and back blue; wings green. Female—same colouring with smaller head, beak and body than male.

Unfortunately, these attractive birds are fairly expensive. Often they are tame or half-tamed as a result of being reared by natives.

Their capacity for imitation is highly praised. Their whole behaviour is calmer and more dignified. A tame bird will perform many little tricks, and enjoys lying on its back.

The birds of this genus do not take to seeds at all readily. Their chief food is nectar.

Black-capped Lories were first bred in England in 1921. One youngster was reared.

Purple-capped Lory (*D. domicella*) Ambon and Ceram

Characteristics: 30 cm (12 in) long. Male—red; black cap; green wings; yellow chest mark and blue shoulder of wing. Female—same colouring with smaller head, beak and body.

It resembles the Black-capped Lory very closely. It likes plenty of opportunities for bathing. It has been bred in Belgium, the United States of America and South Africa.

Chattering Lory (*D. garrula*) Halmahera and several surrounding islands

Characteristics: 31 cm (12¼ in) long. Male—red; green wings; yellow triangular patch on back; bend of wing yellow.

This is the commonest Lory on the market. The variety of races gives plenty of scope for variations in size and colouring. I once had birds with yellow back patches, though some birds do not have this. The latter are smaller and of a darker red.

They are easily excited or upset when a stranger appears.

In my experience, they enjoy sunflower. Many broods have been raised.

Hanging Parrots (*Loriculus*)

Vernal Hanging Parrot *L. vernalis* (2 races)
Philippine Hanging Parrot *L. philippensis* (11 races)
Blue-crowned Hanging Parrot *L. galgulus* (2 races)

Origin and habit: India, Indonesia, Philippines, New Guinea and neighbouring islands. These parrots are only from 11 to 16 cm (4¼–6¼ in) long. They live in dense woods, bamboo forest, on plantations and in orchards. At night they roost like bats.

Their food is nectar, sweet berries, fruits and sugar cane.

They nest in a hollow tree or branch, reasonably close to the ground. Like Lovebirds, they transport nesting material in their feathers. They lay three or four eggs.

General remarks: Thanks to modern transport, Hanging Parrots now reach us in far better condition than formerly. The number of birds imported is never very high, however. Often they are young birds which have not acquired their adult plumage at the time, and only later is it discovered that more males than females have been imported. The Blue-crowned Hanging Parrot is the one most commonly offered for sale. In the early days after their arrival they must be kept at room temperature at the very least. They are tolerant towards other species and do them no harm. The sexes never show any affection towards one another. As skilful runners and climbers, they need plenty of branches, and hard, ridged canes will help to wear the claws down. These beautiful small birds have pleasant voices, twittering and whispering like a songbird.

Feeding: Sweet apples, pears and bananas; some will eat opened figs and boiled rice. Also, softened rusk, soaked sultanas or a mixture of biscuits, chopped-up hard-boiled egg and ants' eggs. Later soaked oats and canary seed can be introduced into their diet. You can also offer mashed potatoes. They like to drink fruit juices meant for babies.

Vernal Hanging Parrot (*L. vernalis*) central and northern India and Thailand

Characteristics: 16 cm (6¼ in) long. Male—green; pale blue throat patch; rump reddish-brown, tail feathers pale blue underneath; beak red. Female—yellowish-green without blue throat patch. Young—no throat patch; dull grey-green plumage.

Housing and rearing. In the house: A cage of at least 70 cm (2 ft 9 in) in length or a bird room are required for this bird. In view of the nature of the food, it is not surprising that most of the excreta is liquid, so keep perches and twigs away from the sides of the cage. This helps to keep the sides of the cage and the floor of the room fairly clean.

Breeding is not easy and has only succeeded a few times prior to the 1970s. A Danish breeder succeeded in raising one youngster. Remarkably enough, his birds nested in a small cardboard box and incubated their eggs for twenty-four days. The birds built their nest from strips of willow bark and reed stems, which they carried to the nest amongst their feathers. The nest box should not be larger than that used for Budgerigars.

The mating display of the male is very interesting. It consists of very peculiar movements and little leaps, and he pretends to feed the end of a twig. Immediately before mating, his wings quiver alarmingly.

In the garden: Once acclimatized, these birds can spend the summer months out of doors. Naturally, they still need a shelter to retreat to in bad weather.

Philippine Hanging Parrot (*L. philippensis*) Philippines

Characteristics: 15 cm (6 in) long. Male—green; red brow and orange throat; green cheeks; golden-yellow nape; beak red. Female—lower throat bluish-yellow and cheeks blue; brow deeper red than male's. Young—green with a red rump; beak at first yellowish; nape shot through with yellow; brow pale red.

Blue-crowned Hanging Parrot (*L. galgulus*) Peninsular Malaysia, Sumatra and Borneo

Characteristics: 13 cm (5 in) long. Male—green; upper head blue; throat and rump red; lower back yellow; beak black. Female—very little blue on the head, no red on throat nor yellow in lower back. Young—as female, lacking blue and red; rump brownish-red; horn-coloured beak.

Housing and rearing. In the house: This species was bred in 1907 in Germany, and has since been reared on a number of occasions. The birds carry leaves to the nest in their feathers. The females lay two or three eggs (rarely four) and incubate them for nineteen to twenty-two days, leaving the nest only occasionally during the day to take food from the male. She alone feeds the young at first. After about four weeks the young leave what is by then a very dirty nest. They are fully moulted at about one year.

In the summer, Blue-crowned Hanging Parrots can be kept out of doors, as long as they have a shelter. In the winter they prefer a constant temperature of 18°C (64°F).

Lovebirds (*Agapornis*)

Abyssinian Lovebird *A. taranta* (2 races)
Madagascar Lovebird *A. cana* (2 races)
Black-collared Lovebird *A. swinderniana* (3 races)
Red-faced Lovebird *A. pullaria* (2 races)
Peach-faced Lovebird *A. roseicollis* (2 races)
Masked Lovebird *A. personata* (4 races)

Origin and habit: Africa, including the Malagasy Republic. Lovebirds live partly in bushy or woodland regions, but also partly in the plains and sandy regions, including mountainous areas up to 3000 metre. They are very agile, hopping and scrambling among the branches, and also clever on the ground. During breeding, they keep in pairs; otherwise they live in small groups.

They build their nests in hollow trees, some species preferring a domed nest, others merely a cup-shaped nest. Some Lovebirds choose the nests of other birds, and others use termite mounds. They line them with bark, pieces of leaves and reeds, transported in their beaks or among their plumage. They feed on seeds, berries and fruits of all kinds.

Lovebirds with white eye rings (*A. personata*) live very close to one another, so it is normal to speak of one main type and several subspecies or geographical races of any one particular region.

General remarks: Lovebirds are very popular and prolific. They do not need a lot of space and many are very pretty. Some, however, have very vicious tempers and have been known to bite off other birds' toes.

They have quiet voices, some species merely chirping like songbirds, but are not usually able to mimic. Sexing is easy with some species, difficult with others. In mature birds in breeding condition, the pelvic bones are a few millimetres apart in females but almost touching in males.

Many varieties fetch about the same price. Lovebirds that are not imported or bred in great quantities are, of course, more expensive. Some types which used to be common are now rarely offered for sale. This is due partly to the cost of expeditions and partly to an export ban by certain African states.

Several colour mutations have been bred and more will probably arise in due course.

Feeding: Sunflower, canary seed, millet, oats, apples and chickweed. In the breeding season plenty of sprouting chickweed or millet, fresh twigs for nest building and chewing. The best sort are thin willow twigs.

Housing and rearing. In the house: A newly-independent Lovebird can grow into a very affectionate and enjoyable house pet. However, its constant companion must not be another bird; it should be a human being who spends plenty of time with him. It is no hardship to spend hours with this little bird because it is so amusing and entertaining. They are very curious and inclined to be playful.

The cage needs to be roomy, and sometimes has to be of metal because some types will eventually destroy wood. If you intend to breed in a cage, it must be at least 60 cm (2 ft) long. You could use a wooden box, lined with metal sheeting to prevent destruction. The birds prefer this because they feel protected since only the front is open for viewing. It is also easier to clean.

Hang a Budgerigar nest box on the inner or outer wall of the cage. Some species need willow, birch or lime twigs for nesting material. The best plan is to stand these in a pot of water to keep them fresh longer. The birds only take moist strips from the twigs, for they need the moisture to help the young to hatch. The young hardly ever emerge when the humidity is low. One pair of Lovebirds can use enormous quantities of damp bark, so if you are unable to provide a regular supply, it is best not to embark on indoor breeding at all. Some types (for example, *A. cana* and *A. taranta*) do not need so much, but they all need plenty of bathing opportunities, as this is another method of introducing moisture into the nest.

You can keep two or three pairs in a loft or larger bird room. It is important, however, that they are all introduced at the same time and when only a few months old, otherwise they will fight.

In the garden: Lovebirds are also ideal subjects for the garden. They need a secluded shelter in which to roost. Newly-imported birds must spend their first winter in a minimum temperature of 15°C (59°F). In the summer, it is best to have nest boxes outside, where it is moister. In the winter, they should be placed in the shelter.

You can keep several pairs in a wooden aviary, as long as they are all placed in it together. Later, remove any surplus males or females. Two birds occupying a nest box are not necessarily a breeding pair; sometimes two males, or two females, pair up. As a rule, however, any superfluous birds sleep alone in a box. You can close up all the entrance holes in the dark, and in the morning discover where the isolated birds are. Of course, you must have enough boxes, all hung at the same height.

From four to six eggs are usual, incubated by the female for twenty-one to twenty-five days, depending on the species. The young leave the nest after four to six weeks and are fed, mainly by the male, for a further two weeks. Once they are independent, remove them, because they will cause problems when the parents breed again and may be attacked by them.

Young birds mature at around ten months. You will always have more females than males. If you are keeping species together, hybridizing may occur. This is not recommended.

Abyssinian Lovebird (*A. taranta*) Ethiopia (illustrated p. 95)

Characteristics: 16 cm (6¼ in) long. Male—green; brow red; beak dark red. Female—no red on head. Young—yellow-brown beak; no red on head until three or four months old; adult colouring at nine months. Small underwing coverts black in males, brown in females.

This Lovebird is found at altitudes of up 3000 metre, so it is the hardiest species, able to withstand even the greatest frosts. Outside breeding time, they go round in groups of up to ten and lead a very nomadic existence, roaming the plains and rarely coming near human habitation.

Abyssinians are imported only sporadically because parts of Ethiopia have export restrictions. They are not in great demand because they are not highly coloured and they are difficult to breed. Some successes have been achieved in cages of 80 cm (2 ft 8 in) in length, and one attempt even succeeded in the winter; here, the birds were released once they had taken to each other and they promptly hid themselves away and were rarely seen. They bred in a starling nest box, without lining the nest, in November in a temperature of only 4°C (39°F). In December snow came, and the temperature dropped to −14°C (7°F)! Nonetheless, the youngsters continued to thrive. The male fed the female and she, in turn, fed the young. Later on, they both took care of feeding the young.

Another breeder has reported that the female carried ivy leaves in her plumage to the nest and ended up with a 'bush' some 3 cm (1¼ in) high. At the start of breeding the Lovebirds attacked the Cockatiels and Redrump Parrakeets they were housed with, biting their legs.

As a rule, they lay three to five eggs and incubate for twenty-four to twenty-five days. Six weeks later the young leave the nest. The parents do not resent being observed during incubation. They have a delicate voice.

Madagascar Lovebird (*A. cana*) Malagasy Republic and neighbouring islands

Characteristics: 13.5 cm (5¼ in) long. Male—green; silver-grey from head to breast. Female—green from head to breast. Young—imported males are all green; domestically reared ones are grey from head to breast but of a slightly darker shade and covering a smaller area than on adult males; beaks partly blackish.

Outside the breeding season, Madagascar Lovebirds live in large groups, though remaining in pairs. They tend to perch on the fringes of woodland and descend into the rice fields and plantations, where they do great damage.

In the past, Madagascar Lovebirds were very common and cheap to buy; nowadays, the Malagasy Republic has banned their export and they have become rarities. Newly-imported specimens are shy and catch cold easily.

It is best to keep them in the house, in a bird room or family room. In a small cage they are rather nervous and this detracts from any pleasure you may have in them. In my experience, they will breed and sleep in a Budgerigar nest box by choice. My birds only used a few sunflower seed husks and two dried leaves as nesting material, but other breeders have reported that their birds used grasses, chickweed, small strips of newspaper, willow bark, pine and larch needles, cranberry and other leaves. They have also been known to construct a domed nest out of straw.

A clutch almost always consists of four to five eggs, which the female incubates for twenty-two days. Almost five weeks later, the young leave the nest. Young males emerge with a silver-grey head, whereas imported young males have a green head. This could be a case of captivity leading to the emission of a moult, as is known to be the case with other birds.

Once the young have emerged from the nest it is the male who takes care of them because the female immediately becomes broody again. My youngsters were reared almost exclusively on a diet of millet. They overwinter in the cold weather as long as it remains frost free. Some breeders have suffered no losses when the temperature went as low as −9°C (16°F) but this can only apply to birds reared here, or at least ones which are very well acclimatized. It is not a good idea to house them with another species.

Black-collared Lovebird (*A. swinderniana*) Cameroons, Liberia and the Congo

Characteristics: 13 cm (5 in) long. Male and female—green; breast olive-yellow; black ring on nape; upper tail feathers blue; root of tail red; beak blackish; iris orange-yellow. Young—no black ring; paler beak.

No living Black-collared Lovebirds have ever reached Europe, as far as is known. They are exclusively birds of the woods, feeding off figs and rice.

Red-faced Lovebird (*A. pullaria*) Sierra Leone, Cameroons, northern Angola, Uganda and Rwanda (illustrated p. 95)

Characteristics: 14 cm (5½ in) long. Male—green; crimson from top of head, across cheeks to upper throat; rump blue; undertail coverts black; beak red. Female—paler red head; undertail coverts green. Young—brow and surrounding area yellowish; beak pale red. Young males in the nest already show black undertail coverts.

After World War II, Red-faced Lovebirds were quite common and reasonably priced; now, they are no longer available on the open market.

They are at home in thickly wooded regions. Their sole food is grass seeds and millet, but they will take wild figs on occasion.

Their choice of nest site is very peculiar—they prefer termite mounds or the nests of tree ants. The latter resemble sponges because they are constructed out of leaves which the ants have chewed into holes. The Red-faced Lovebirds dig their way into these structures or termite nests without being attacked by the ants. Nests have also been found in the trunk of a tree fern. They lay five to seven eggs.

Because of the peculiarity of their nest site, Red-faced Lovebirds have very rarely been bred in captivity. Numerous attempts have been made to encourage them to breed. In England, damp turf was packed into small barrels and the birds tunnelled a nest into it. One youngster hatched in October but it died thirty-five days later when there was a sudden drop in the temperature. In Cape Town, pieces of cork measuring $50 \times 40 \times 20$ cm (1 ft 8 in $\times$ $15\frac{3}{4}$ in $\times$ 8 in) were fixed in the branches, and holes measuring 5 cm (2 in) in diameter were bored into them. The birds enlarged the holes for themselves and sixteen days later a female was sitting. This method was successful for two breeders and they were able to rear several young. They left the nest after about thirty days. In each case, the successes took place in a very large aviary, occupied by only one pair. E. Zürcher, in Ostermundingen in Switzerland, had failed broods for four years, until finally being successful in 1975/76.

Young birds are very suitable for cages. As single birds, they grow very tame and only ever make a chirping, songbird-like noise.

Peach-faced Lovebird (*A. roseicollis*) south-west Africa (illustrated p. 95)

Characteristics: 17 cm ($6\frac{3}{4}$ in) long. Male—green; brow, head, neck and throat pink; rump bright blue; flesh-coloured beak. Female—bigger; paler colouring on head. Young—blackish beak and duller pink colouring.

Peach-faced Lovebirds inhabit the dry areas on the fringes of deserts. However, they must always be within reach of a watering place. Outside the breeding season, they go around in flocks, making a loud 'tsick-tsick' noise. They feed on all kinds of berries and seeds.

These small parrots nest in decayed tree trunks or take over nests abandoned by the Colonial Sparrow or Mahali Weaver. All three species have been known to live peacefully with one another.

Peach-faced Lovebirds are always available through the trade at a very attractive price. Even imported birds are hardy.

A single young bird is ideal for keeping in the house. It quickly becomes tame and attaches itself to its owner. However, only undertake to keep your Peach-faced Lovebird in the room with you if you can bear its harsh voice, which is hardly ever silent. Two birds kept together will encourage each other to be noisy.

In the garden, however, they are ideal, breeding readily for many seasons and producing many offspring. It is not always easy to sex these birds. Females have their feet much further apart than the males; they are also larger. When the birds are ready for breeding, at about seven to nine months, you can feel their pelvic bones. In males, these are virtually touching, whereas in females there is always a small space between them. One other possibility is to put several young in an aviary at one time and let them choose their own mates. You can remove superfluous birds later. Never put new birds in with an old pair as this always leads to fights.

Only females transport pieces of bark among their feathers for nest linings. When this method of carrying nesting material was first observed, in 1869, it caused a sensation. Pieces of bark, preferably from willows, birches or lime trees, are normally 6–8 cm (2¼–3 in) long and carried five or seven at a time by the female to the nest. They are used to build a domed nest. The entrance is at the top, on one side, only the rear wall being left fairly open. For this reason, it is a good idea to make the back of your nest box removable for inspection during incubation.

The female incubates her three to five eggs for twenty-two days. The young leave the nest after five or six weeks and are immediately very skilful and accurate fliers. The father feeds them for the next two weeks because the female lays again straight away. As soon as the young are independent, it is wise to remove them because otherwise their parents could attack them. Try to avoid more than three broods a year.

Peach-faced Lovebirds can overwinter in an unheated shelter. There is no special food for breeding; just make sure that dandelion, chickweed or lettuce are always available. Sprouting millet spray is especially good.

Mutations: A blue mutation has been observed in the wild. This has also occurred in captivity. However, it is really a blue-green colour, in no way to be compared with the blue of the Masked Lovebird (*A. p. personata*). This factor is genetically recessive. A yellow form was first reared in Japan and South Africa; they are of a canary-yellow colour with the pink head of the original form, and are sometimes called Golden Cherry Lovebirds. Genetic inheritance of yellow and pied birds is recessive. (In 1975 albinos were bred in Holland and the USA.)

Birds with many red patches are also known of. This, however, is not a mutation and cannot be inherited; it is merely an aberration.

115

Masked Lovebird (*A. personata personata*) northern Tanzania (illustrated p. 96)

Characteristics: 16 cm (6¼ in) long. Male and female—green; head black; nape, throat and breast yellow; white eye ring; beak red. Young—head a paler brown-black; dull yellow; base of beak blackish. First moult at around eight or nine months.

The four races of Lovebirds with white eye rings are all concentrated in a relatively small area. Not only do they have the white eye rings in common; they also carry their nesting material in their beaks.

Masked Lovebirds live in the grasslands where acacias and mimosa bushes flourish. Flocks of twenty to forty birds haunt the river banks but avoid the real highlands. They feed on grass and other seeds, as well as berries. They nest in hollow tree trunks.

These Lovebirds are always available from traders or breeders, and are amongst the most popular. Sexing them is not easy—use the same guidelines as given for the Peach-faced. Also observe their behaviour; the male adopts a more upright stance and rarely goes into the nest box; he also has a narrower eye ring. They often scratch their heads with a foot, especially just before mating occurs. Only the female lines the nest, and her eye ring is broader all round. Females are also larger and heavier.

A single youngster kept in a cage soon becomes trusting. Its voice is less harsh than that of the Peach-faced. Breeding has often proved successful, in a cage of 80 cm (1 ft 8 in) long. It is always wise to keep your birds as pairs, never more together, since otherwise fights break out.

However, it is quite possible to keep several birds together in an aviary, provided that they are all introduced into it at the same time and whilst still quite young. If you cannot do this, keep an established pair isolated to prevent attacks on newcomers.

This is another occasion when it is useful to hang up more nest boxes than there are pairs. Make sure that there is a plentiful and constant supply of willow twigs because the birds use an enormous quantity of these in building their domed nests and the moisture that the twigs provide is very important during incubation.

As for all Lovebirds with white eye rings, incubation lasts twenty-one to twenty-three days and the young remain on the nest for four to five weeks.

These small parrots can withstand a few degrees of frost, as long as they have boxes to retire to at night. Of course, newly-imported birds will need to be maintained at room temperature during their first winter here. They are somewhat delicate at first and need time to acclimatize themselves.

Mutations: The blue mutation of the Masked was first captured in 1927. Nowadays they are bred fairly successfully not only in Japan, Taiwan, Hong Kong and the USA, but also in Europe.

When breeding, it is not a good idea to pair blue with blue continually; occasionally, cross a blue with a normal-coloured specimen to improve the quality of the blues bred (illustrated p. 96).

blue × blue = all blue birds
blue × normal = all normal, some of which are split for blue
blue × split blue = approx. half blue and half split blue
plit blue × split blue = approx. half split, a quarter blue and a quarter
normal

You can identify blues when they are still in the nest because they have white down, whereas normals have reddish down. An adult blue is blue where the normally-coloured bird is green; grey-white instead of yellow; the beak is bright red.

Further mutations include yellows and whites but the names are misleading because the birds are not pure yellow or pure white.

There has also been a grey-winged mutation, produced by yellows and whites. Its head and primaries are virtually white. I also know of cinnamon-coloured Masked Lovebirds in Japan.

Fischer's Lovebird (*A. personata fischeri*) north-west Tanzania (illustrated p. 96)

Characteristics: 16 cm (6¼ in) long. Male and female—brow, cheeks and throat orange; back of head olive green; nape yellow; breast orange-yellow; upper parts green; white eye ring; uppertail coverts blue; beak red. Young—duller colours.

Fischer's Lovebird is more sociable and tolerant than the Masked and better behaved with other birds. Take care to acquire good, thoroughbred specimens with clear, bright colours. Everything else relevant to this bird has been covered under the Masked.

Mutations: Reports have come from California of a blue Fischer's. It is said to have sky blue plumage and a white-grey head. Yellow Fischer's are rare; they are genetically recessive.

Nyasa Lovebird (*A. personata lilianae*) Northern Zimbabwe to Malawi (illustrated p. 96)

Characteristics: 14 cm (5½ in). Male and female—brow, crown, sides of head and throat scarlet; nape olive green; upper parts green; white eye ring. Uppertail coverts *green* and beak red. Female—body, head and beak somewhat sturdier. (Note position of pelvic bones.) Young—duller colouring.

Sadly, this race has become much rarer in recent years, due to export restrictions in Nyasaland.

Nyasas are smaller than Fischer's Lovebird and have all green upper plumage on the tail. If they have just a few blue feathers there, it shows that they have Fischer's Lovebirds in their ancestry.

Often you can only tell the sexes by their behaviour. They are noted for their very peaceable attitude towards each other and also towards other psittacines. I kept several pairs very happily in a flight measuring some 4 m (13 ft) long. Of all Lovebirds with white eye rings, Nyasas are the most difficult to breed. They lay a high proportion of infertile eggs and the mortality rate amongst both nestlings and adults is high. They need to be kept free from frost and at a temperature never lower than 10°C (50°F) during the winter.

Mutations: Yellow and Lutino Nyasas are very rare, probably only found in California.

Black-cheeked Lovebird (*A. personata nigrigensis*) Northern Zimbabwe (illustrated p. 96)

Characteristics: 14.5 cm (5¾ in) long. Male and female—upper head and cheeks dark brown; rear of head and sides of throat yellow-green; throat orange-brown; upper parts dark green; white eye ring; red beak. Young—duller.

Black-cheeked Lovebirds have also become rarer recently. Pure-bred birds have no black on the head, no yellow on the throat and no blue in the uppertail coverts. They are smaller than the Nyasas and, like them, can be sexed according to their behaviour. They are friendly towards their own kind and other birds. Some exceptional breeding pairs yield three broods a year.

Birds bred here are able to tolerate a few degrees of frost but imported specimens have to be kept at 15°C (59°F) or more, otherwise substantial losses will occur, as described for Masked Lovebirds.

Parrotlets (*Forpus*)

Turquoise-rumped Parrotlet *F. cyanopygius* (3 races)
Green-and Blue-rumped Parrotlet *F. passerinus* (11 races)
Sclater's Parrotlet *F. sclateri* (2 races)
Celestial Parrotlet *F. coelestis*
Spectacled Parrotlet *F. conspicillatus* (3 races)

Origin and habit: Mexico, Colombia, Venezuela, Guyana, Ecuador, Peru, Brazil and Paraguay. America's smallest parrots are only 12 to 14 cm (4¾–5½ in) long. Their wings are longer than their wedge-shaped tails. They live in woody areas but avoid the thick rain forests. Parrotlets go around in colonies and feed on seeds, berries and fruits. They do not use their feet for feeding.

They breed in hollow trees or branches, and also in holes in the ground or Ovenbird nests. A clutch consists of three to seven eggs, but eight or nine are not unusual.

General remarks: Some species appear sporadically in great numbers on the market and others are seldom offered for sale. Imported specimens are shy and are not easy to acclimatize. You have to keep such birds at room temperature. In my experience, they suffer from a tendency to catch cold in the early days and this often becomes chronic and occasionally fatal. Birds bred here are completely different; they are not at all sensitive and can become extremely tame. They have a quiet voice, ideal for sharing a room. You know which sex you are buying as this can be determined in the nest.

Feeding: Canary seed, spray millet, oats, small sunflower, white millet; also, apples and carrots, soaked figs, chickweed, sorrel and dandelion. For breeding, add soaked white bread or chopped-up hard-boiled egg, sprouting millet or oats, biscuits and dried insect food. Crushed egg-shells are a good source of calcium. Parrotlets need far more food than their size would lead you to expect.

Housing and rearing. In the house: Parrotlets can be kept in a cage quite happily. Very young or hand-reared birds taken from the nest can become very tame. They learn to speak, sneeze, laugh and imitate all sorts of sounds. If you want one like this, however, you will have to restrict yourself to keeping only one bird and spend a great deal of time with it.

For breeding, you must have no more than one pair in a cage that measures at least 50 cm (1 ft 8 in) long. Imported birds are better in a box with an open front, set at about eye-level. This gives them more peace and a greater feeling of security. The nest box, normally Budgerigar-sized, can be fixed either inside or outside the cage. Some types prefer an upright nest, others a horizontal one. Place a layer of peat or wood shavings on the bottom. Some Parrotlets collect bark and use that. The usual clutch is four to six eggs, sometimes eight or nine. One egg is laid every thirty-five to forty-eight hours. The female sits for nineteen to twenty-one days, guarded by her male. If he gives an alarm-call, she leaves the nest. The young leave the nest after about four weeks and continue to be fed by their parents for a further twelve to eighteen days. Once you have a good breeding pair, two or three broods are not uncommon. However, there are occasionally pairs which never breed. The only thing to do in that case is to exchange one of the partners, as it is clear that, for one reason or another, they are not compatible.

Birds bred here can safely overwinter without heating. They get on with other species to varying degrees. Green-rumps are generally more tolerant than Blue-rumps. Keeping them in cages or bird rooms with finches often works well, apart from a few biting incidents during the breeding season.

In the garden: All types can be kept in the garden in the summer. They must have access to a dry, draught-free shelter. In winter this should be as frost-free as possible. Breeding in an aviary is easier than in an indoor cage. Newly-imported specimens should only be let out in good weather to join the birds in the aviary. Otherwise, see under *In the house.*

Turquoise-rumped Parrotlet (*F. cyanopygius*) Mexico (illustrated p. 129)

Characteristics: 13 cm (5 in) long. Male—yellow-green; rump and fore-edges of wing blue; underwing coverts dark blue. Female—wings dull green. Young—duller. Sexing possible in the nest.

Green- and Blue-rumped Parrotlet (*F. passerinus*) Colombia, Venezuela, Guyana, Peru, Brazil and Paraguay (illustrated p. 129)

Characteristics: 13 cm (5 in) long. Male—green; underparts yellow-green; rump green; underwing coverts blue; primaries and secondaries blue. Female—underwing coverts dull green. Young—duller colours. Sexing possible while still in the nest.

Five races of this species have *green rumps* and six more or less *bluish rumps.*

Sclater's Parrotlet (*F. sclateri*) eastern Ecuador, eastern Peru, eastern Venezuela, Guyana and western Brazil.

Characteristics: 12 cm (4¾ in) long. Male—dark green; rump, secondaries and underwing coverts blue; beak lead blue, whitish underneath. Female—rump and underwing coverts green.

Less frequently imported; sometimes not even recognized for what it is.

Celestial Parrotlet (*F. coelestis coelestis*) Ecuador and Peru (illustrated p. 129)

Characteristics: 12 cm (4¾ in) long. Male—green; blue band above the eye; pale blue nape, rump, underwing coverts and secondaries; front and sides of head yellowish-green; back grey-green. Female—green; no blue tints. Young—duller; sexing possible in the nest.

Forpus xanthops from northern Peru has a yellow face and is therefore named the Yellow-faced Celestial Parrotlet.

Spectacled Parrotlet (*F. conspicillatus*) Colombia

Characteristics: 12 cm (4¾ in) long. Male—green; rump, secondaries and primaries blue; blue eye-ring. Female—rump, primaries and secondaries green. Young—green, but young males already show blue edges to their primaries in the nest, whereas young females are all green.

This beautiful little parrot was first introduced in Europe in 1973. At first, importers did not recognize them to be this species.

Housing and rearing. In the house: Mature birds are extremely tame and give a great deal of pleasure. Breeding should have priority because of the small numbers in captivity. My first youngsters were born in May 1974 (one other breeder had his first success in the same year). The female lays three to five eggs and remains completely out of sight during the incubation period. Whenever there is the slightest disturbance, and also at night, the male also takes to the nest.

For breeding, they enjoy sprouting seeds, soaked figs, greenfood (chickweed), rowan berries, medlar and soft food.

Brotogeris Parrakeets

All Green Parrakeet *B. tirica*
White-winged Parrakeet *B. versicolorus* (3 races)
Orange-flanked Parrakeet *B. pyrrhopterus*
Bee Bee Parrot/Tovi Parrakeet *B. jugularis* (3 races)

Origin and habit: Central and South America. Huge swarms of *Brotogeris* Parrakeets inhabit the warm coastal regions, woods and scrublands. They flock to the plantations and plunder the crops of rice, fruit and maize. They do everything together—feeding, chattering, drinking. This makes it very easy to catch large numbers of them with nets. You find their nests in holes in trees, containing three to five eggs. They live as pairs during the breeding season.

General remarks: The small Parrakeets of this genus are between 17 and 25 cm (6¾–9¾ in) long. The birds are a fairly uniform green and there is not much difference between the colouring of the sexes. Behaviour offers no clues, since two males or two females will pair up just as readily as a breeding pair. Some types are frequently on the market at a favourable price. They have very strong voices which can get on one's nerves. Youngsters can become extremely tame, and some kept as isolated birds make very little disturbing noise. All species sleep in nest boxes at night. They must be protected from frost during the winter.

Feeding: Canary seed, millet, small sunflower, oats, apples, carrots and chickweed; sprouting seedlings during the breeding season.

All-green Parrakeet (*B. tirica*) eastern and southern Brazil (illustrated p. 130)

Characteristics: 25 cm (9¾ in) long. Male—green; nape and tail feathers bluish; beak pale flesh colour. Female—dull grey-green.

Housing and rearing: The All-green Parrakeet is the largest *Brotogeris* and has been reared in a cage. The female lays five eggs, one every second day, and sits for about twenty-two days. The young birds leave the nest after six weeks but rush back to it at the slightest disturbance. The parents object to being observed during incubation. My birds fed on biscuits, hard-boiled egg chopped-up, and millet during breeding.

It is said that seventy years ago a blue mutation was reared in the castle at Schönbrunn, near Vienna.

Canary-winged Parrakeet (*B. versicolorus chiriri*) Bolivia, Brazil and Paraguay

Characteristics: 22 cm (8¾ in) long. Male and female—green; large yellow patch on the secondaries.

This parrot is a race of the White-winged Parrakeet (*B. v. versicolorus*). *Housing and rearing. In the house:* A single Canary-winged Parrakeet can become very tame, but its loud voice can be something of a trial. Some of them learn a few words. Not many attempts at breeding have succeeded.

Orange-flanked Parrakeet (*B. pyrrhopterus*) western South America, from Ecuador to north-west Peru

Characteristics: 21 cm (8¼ in) long. Male and female—green; sides of head, chin and brow greyish; crown blue-green; secondaries and underwing coverts orange.

Housing and rearing. In the house: This Parrakeet can become very tame and affectionate. It does not make much use of its voice, a point to recommend it. A few breeding successes have occurred. In one case four eggs were laid and incubated for about twenty-six days. After about six weeks the young emerged from the nest. Some Orange-flanks have been known to imitate a few words.

In the garden: It has been reported that two Orange-flanks came through two harsh winters unharmed in an outdoor shelter which was not heated. Of course, there must be a box for them to roost in. They were trained to fly free once a strong pair bond had been established.

Bee Bee Parrot/Tovi Parrakeet (*B. jugularis*) Mexico to northern Colombia, northern Venezuela and northern Peru (illustrated p. 130)

Characteristics: 18 cm (7 in) long. Male and female—green; orange patch on chin; small pinions golden brown; secondaries blue.

Housing and rearing. In the house: Even though this bird has a very plain appearance, it can still become a well-loved companion. It can even be so tame that it is a nuisance, following its owner's every move and always wanting to sit on his shoulders. You have to be very careful not to shut one in a door. Even birds caught at an advanced age grow tame when they are the only bird you keep and if you devote plenty of time to them. The voice is not loud or unpleasant. Newly-imported birds have to be maintained at room temperature, and they need a box for the night to keep them out of draughts. Tovis have been bred on a number of occasions. The nest box provided should be the same size as one for Budgerigars. They only need a layer of peat or wood shavings.

Quaker Parrakeets (*Myiopsitta*)

Quaker Parrakeet (*M. monachus*)

Characteristics: 29 cm (11½ in) long. Male and female—grey-green; brow, front of head, cheeks, throat and upper breast grey with dark wavy shading; secondaries blue; all other plumage greenish. Young—not such a bright green; head dull green; iris dark; less obvious wavy shading; flights more green than blue; tail feathers shorter.

Origin and habit: Bolivia to Uruguay and eastern Argentina. The Quaker Parrakeet inhabits the moist regions and is also found in the mountains up to 1000 metre. They spend the whole year in colonies, including the breeding seasons. Huge flocks descend on the fruit and maize fields, destroying more than they can eat. The 'Calita', as the natives call it, builds a spherical nest in the high trees. They construct colonial nests, often up to 2–3 m (6 ft 6 in–9 ft 9 in) tall, which are shared by several pairs. Quite often, they fall out of the trees because they are so heavy. Occasionally they take over an old predator's nest and build on that.

General remarks: The Quaker Parrakeet is a very interesting bird. It is the only parrot which builds its nest out of twigs. On the ground it is very clumsy, but in the branches it is quite agile. Quakers are imported in large quantities, so you will always find them for sale at a reasonable price. The plumage is fairly plain and the voice quite loud. Because of these attributes, it is kept mainly in aviaries or flying free.

Feeding: Sunflower, oats, canary seed, millet, partially ripe corn on the cob, ground nuts, and fruit. For breeding, old soaked white bread, plenty of lettuce and spinach beet.

Housing and rearing. In the house: Because of their loud voices, Quaker Parrakeets are not recommended for the house. Quakers are destructive and gnaw everything within reach. If you want a pet, you should only obtain a young bird, which is capable of imitating a few words and sounds.

In the garden: It is possible to keep these birds in an aviary, despite the above-mentioned drawbacks. Because they roost in colonies, it is possible to keep

K.A. Uder's Quaker Parrakeets in Adendorf even built their nest of twigs on the ground.

several pairs in one flight, but it is not advisable to keep them with another species. Their lives and pursuits are fascinating to watch. Put a base (such as stout timbers, crossed) in a sheltered corner for them to build their nest on; the right sort of twigs must also be available. The male takes sticks, up to the thickness of a pencil, to the female who constructs the nest with them. Some of the twigs can be up to 50 cm (20 in) long. They put a roof on the nest, so that the final structure resembles a sphere. The entrance tunnel is to one side or pointing downwards. This is to protect them from unwelcome visitors, such as tree snakes. The actual nest is lined with grasses. The entrance is guarded by the male, the female remaining almost totally hidden throughout the incubation. The birds stick to their home winter and summer. If it is damaged by a storm, they set to and repair it. They also take twigs into a large nest box and build a base with them. It can take up to three months to build such a nest. It is unusual to find a nest on the ground. They breed readily, two broods each of four to six young being normal. It is difficult to determine the actual length of the incubation as the female takes to the nest quite early on and it is virtually impossible to see inside the nest to check up on its contents. It is difficult to tell the sexes apart, though behaviour offers some clues here. The best policy is to acquire several birds and remove the superfluous ones once pairing has taken place. This way, you can build up a proper breeding colony.

Quaker Parrakeets are ready for breeding at one year of age. They have been known to get on well sharing an aviary with Peach-faced Lovebirds.

Since their beaks are very strong, do not use any thin wire netting, and wood is not very practical, either. An iron structure is preferable. The sheltering walls and the roof must also be of some stout material, such as concrete or stone. They are unaffected by cold, tolerating −25°C (−13°F) well in their nests.

Free flight: Since these birds are closely bound to their nests the whole year through, they are ideally suited as liberty birds. They will always return, so, as soon as they have completed their nests, it is safe to remove the netting. You then have a free flying colony of Quaker Parrakeets. Naturally, you must consider the neighbours; they will not enjoy having their fruit trees plundered. Even when the birds are not the least bit hungry, they still enjoy picking off the apples, pears and cherries and dropping them to the ground. They will also chew the twigs and branches. I would only advise people living in isolated houses in wooded areas to keep Quakers at liberty. Trials have shown that the birds will wander up to some 6 km (3 miles) from their place of origin. Occasionally birds will fall victim to a predator or hunter. The birds need a regular supply of fresh twigs to repair their nests.

Mutations: Yellow and blue mutations have been offered for sale, both at high prices however.

Aymara Parrakeets (*Amoropsittaca*)

Aymara Parrakeet (*A. aymara*)

Characteristics: 20 cm (8 in) long. Male—green; head brown-grey; cheeks and front of throat grey; underparts yellowish-green. Female—smaller; grey on cheeks is paler.

Origin and habit: Bolivia, northern Chile, northern Argentina. This small Parrakeet was named after a tribe of Indians, the Aymaras. It is found at an altitude of up to 2600 metre, where the nights can be really cold. In such regions only cacti grow, so they nest in sandy banks or clefts in the rocks, or holes in the ground.

General remarks: Nothing was known about this Parrakeet until it was first imported into Europe around 1960. Then quite a substantial number came over and were offered for sale at a very reasonable price. It is rarely available, but is an ideal aviary bird due to its quiet, unassuming nature and very melodious voice.

Feeding: Sunflower, hemp, wild bird food, canary seed, spray millet, apples, carrots, chickweed, spinach, shepherd's purse. They love to gnaw fresh shoots of elderberry.

For breeding add germinating sunflower and partially-ripe corn. They sometimes take to a softfood—chopped-up hard-boiled egg mixed to a porridge with rusks.

Housing and rearing. In the house: Aymaras are particularly well-suited to cage rearing. A young bird kept singly will quickly grow tame and confiding. You should furnish it with a Budgerigar nestbox as it likes to spend the night there.

Breeding has succeeded in an 80 cm (2 ft 8 in) long cage. They have been known to lay ten eggs, one every two days. Incubation seems to have taken about twenty days but I cannot be sure of this in view of the large size of the clutch. You hardly ever see the female the whole time. The male spends only part of the day on the nest but he is at the hen's side through the night. They do not mind you checking up on them as they sit. The young begin to emerge from the nest after five weeks. At dusk, it is the youngsters who enter the nest box first. They are so trusting that they will happily sit on your finger.

In the garden: Aymaras are just as at home in the garden, as long as they have a shelter. Some people say that they even wanted to go out into the flight in the winter. Since they are naturally birds of the higher regions, this insensitivity to cold is understandable. One other advantage is that they always go into the box voluntarily at night and are thus protected from the cold or from any disturbance. Breeding succeeds better in an aviary than in a cage.

Experience has shown that this Parrakeet gets on very well with Budgerigars, all types of finches and Softbills.

Lineolated Parrakeets (*Bolborhynchus*)

Lineolated Parrakeet (*B. lineola*, 3 races) (illustrated p. 130)

Characteristics: 17 cm (6¾ in) long. Male—green; underparts yellow-green; upperparts and sides barred horizontally black; paler beak. Female—smaller; fewer narrow black-edged feathers. Young—plumage, beak and feet paler than adults'.

Origin and habit: Mexico, Panama, Colombia and Peru. This genus inhabits the stony, almost treeless wildernesses, up to altitudes of 2000 metre. They are good runners and try to escape danger by pressing themselves, motionless, close to the ground. Their food is grass and weed seeds. Their nests are found in old dead trees.

General remarks: Only limited numbers of the Lineolated Parrakeet are imported. It has a very pleasant voice and a gentle temperament. Imported birds can, however, be rather shy.

Feeding: Sunflower, canary seed, millet, dandelion leaves, lettuce, cherries, pears and, for breeding, soaked and squeezed-out stale white bread mixed with chopped-up hard-boiled egg.

Housing and rearing. In the house: A young bird kept alone in a cage will slowly become tame and will even learn to imitate a few words, though not very many. You will need to provide a nest box for roosting. Breeding has been known to succeed in a cage only 60 cm (2 ft) long. The brood box was 25 × 15 × 15 cm (9¾ × 8 × 8 in) and the entrance hole was 8 cm (3 in) in diameter. Since most Lineolated Parrakeets do without a nest as such, you only need a shallow layer of peat or wood shavings, about two fingers' depth, on the bottom of the box. A clutch usually numbers four or five eggs, incubated for twenty-two or twenty-three days by the female. The male appears to be very involved in the whole affair and feeds both the female and the youngsters. They do not mind you checking up on them from time to time. The young leave the nest after four or five weeks and are independent at around six or seven weeks. The whole family continue to use the nest box as a night-time refuge. By the time they are two months old, there is hardly any difference between the youngsters and their parents.

In the garden: Lineolateds are also suitable for aviaries. In Holland they have overwintered without heating and then bred. They get on well with Bourke's Parrakeets, Cockatiels, Plum-head Parrakeets and Finches.

Patagonian Conures (*Cyanoliseus*)

Lesser Patagonian Conure (*C. patagonus*, 3 races) (illustrated p. 131)

Characteristics: 45 cm (17¾ in) long. Male and female—olive brown; belly dirty yellow with a red patch.

Origin and habit: Argentina, Chile and Uruguay. The Patagonian Conure lives far south of the equator. Since winters there are very cold and unpleasant, they migrate north in the cold months, as far as Uruguay. They live in colonies in the rocky parts of the Andes and Cordilleras where there are ample hollows and crevices for them to hide and nest in. There are no trees here. They occasionally excavate tunnels in the limestone or stony ground and make a nest where the three eggs are laid. They stay in colonies during breeding. They feed on weed seeds, corn and berries.

General remarks: These Conures are occasionally on sale but they are not very popular. People are put off by their loud voices, great desire to chew things, difficulty in breeding and not very attractive appearance. Also, prices are usually high.

Feeding: Sunflower and other seeds, peanuts and apples.

Housing and rearing. In the house: For the above-mentioned reasons, keeping them in the house is not recommended.

In the garden: The Lesser Patagonian Conure is a hardy bird, well able to withstand our climate. Since they are such inveterate chewers, you must build the aviary out of metal and use extremely strong wire netting. They are good on the ground but poor climbers. Thus, one or two thick branches are better than a lot of twigs.

A few years ago, what must have been the first breeding success of the larger race took place in England. The birds bred in a nest box, laying three eggs which they incubated for about twenty-five days.

Macaws (*Ara*), Blue Macaws (*Anodorhynchus*)

Macaws

Illiger's Macaw *A. maracana*
Severe Macaw *A. severa* (2 races)
Scarlet Macaw *A. macao*
Green-winged Macaw *A. chloroptera*
Military Macaw *A. militaris* (4 races)
Blue and Gold Macaw *A. ararauna*

Blue Macaws

Hyacinthine Macaw *Anodorhynchus hyacinthinus*

Origin and habit: I have often been asked why Macaws should sometimes be known as Arara, instead of Ara, their Latin name. It is because their territory is shared by an Indian tribe of that name. The remaining few members of this tribe live around the Amazon, and in the province of Mato Grosso, where the River Xingu rises. It was reported at the beginning of 1976 that three government geologists were killed by some Arara Indians.

Macaws are found from Mexico to Brazil's southern tip. The largest parrots in the world live in tropical America. All along the banks of the rivers,

Page 129
Top left: Turquoise-rumped Parrotlet (*Forpus cyanopygius*)
Top right: Green-rumped Parrotlet (*Forpus passerinus*)
Bottom: Celestial Parrotlet (*Forpus coelestis coelestis*)

Page 130
Top left: Bee Bee Parrot/Tovi Parrakeet (*Brotogeris jugularis*)
Top right: All-Green Parrakeet (*Brotogeris tirica*)
Bottom: Lineolated Parrakeet (*Bolborhynchus lineola*)

Page 131
Top left: Military Macaw (*Ara ambigua*)
Top right: Lesser Patagonian Conure (*Cyanoliseus patagonus*)
Bottom left: *Left*, Green-winged Macaw (*Ara chloroptera*); *right*, Scarlet Macaw (*Ara macao*)
Bottom right: Hyacinthine Macaw (*Anodorhyncus hyacinthus*)

Page 132
Top left: Sun/Yellow Conure (*Aratinga solstitialis*)
Top right: Golden-crowned Conure (*Aratinga aurea*)
Bottom: Nanday Conure (*Nandayus nenday*)

they are the characteristic jungle birds. Their only enemy is man. Nevertheless, one species has become extinct. Some types live up to 3000 metre above sea level. They are very ungainly on the ground. Their nests have to be in large holes, so they are restricted to certain regions. Pairs return to the same nest site year after year. The natives claimed these trees for their own, and passed them on through the family as an inheritance, for Macaws have always been popular pets with them. They used their feathers as adornments. They would take the youngsters from the nests and tame them.

Macaws in the wild feed on berries, fruits and corn. They can do great damage to plantations. Outside the breeding season, they go around in flocks, but the pairs always remain together. Two eggs are laid and incubated by the female alone. When the young are hungry, they drum against the sides of the hollow tree to make this fact known.

General remarks: The specimens which reach Europe are almost all half-tame birds, either caught when young or reared by hand. They have another advantage in that they very quickly adapt to their new surroundings; being kept chained to perches in zoos, for example. I still cannot recommend this form of treatment, however. Unfortunately, they have to put up with a lot of teasing in zoos; luckily, not many specimens are bad-tempered. When they are angry, they raise their crown feathers and their white cheeks become tinged with pink.

The voice sounds rather like 'ara'. You only stand a chance of training a young bird to give this noise up. They are quick to learn a few words but rarely achieve little sentences. Macaws can become part of the family and often live to the ripe old age of a hundred.

Feeding: Various nuts, sunflower, maize or corn on the cob, wheat and oats, apples and other fruit, carrots, rusks and fresh twigs to chew. You must offer as varied a diet as possible.

Housing and rearing. In the house: There are two ways to keep a Macaw in the house—in a cage or on a stand. When you are not present, and overnight, the bird can be caged; the cage must be very large—at least $1.5 \times 1.5 \times 1.5$ m $(5 \times 5 \times 5$ ft). By day it can be kept on a stand, without a chain. Since every bird is different, it is up to the owner how much freedom he allows an individual bird to have. Of course, the cage must be of metal and very strong, and the stand must be made of a very stout branch of beech or oak, as thick as your arm. On no account use a metal perch as this always leads to foot ailments. You must also realize that in time even hardwood will be chewed through if you fail to provide enough extra wood specially for chewing. The bark contains nutrients which are vital to these large psittacines. It is only thus, and with a very varied diet, that your Macaw will grow a really splendid plumage. It is absolutely essential to spray your bird every day.

A newly-arrived bird should be put into a cage. Gradually you will get to know each other and when you think your bird is settled and mature enough, you can introduce him to his stand. Since they are primarily climbing, not flying, birds, Macaws only leave the stand when they are really frightened. As time goes by, he will no longer feel the need to leave it. If you really cannot manage without a chain, this must have at least two swivels to prevent it from tangling up. If the chain is too thin, the bird will easily bite through it; if it is too thick, it will become too heavy for the bird. Change the chain to the other leg from time to time to rest the leg and prevent swellings. None of these arrangements is really ideal.

Within the family circle, a Macaw will have its favourite, be it the husband, wife or child. If you are the chosen one, you will be able to take what liberties you like with the bird with impunity; if not, watch out for its large beak, which can be dangerous on occasions.

In the garden: You can, of course, keep Macaws in a flight in the garden. Both aviary and shelter must be constructed out of some very strong material. Macaws are not troubled by the cold but you still have to protect them from frost because their feet are easily damaged. Some are territorial, so it is possible to keep them flying free, as long as you have the right sort of environment. You could also construct a walled-in enclosure so that a bird with *one* clipped wing would not be able to get out. You must put the right sort of climbing tree in the enclosure. Tame birds can also be kept in the garden on a perch. The sunshine or the occasional shower will do them good.

Most species have been bred successfully, in particular the dwarf Macaws. They do not need much space. The problem is sexing Macaws. We do not know at what age they become sexually mature, and with the larger types you just have to wait and see. Details about known breeding successes are given under the various types.

Macaws

Illiger's Macaw (*A. maracana*) eastern Brazil

Characteristics: 44 cm (17¼ in) long. Male—green; brow, lower back and v-shaped patch on belly dark red; head slightly bluish; tail reddish-brown with blue tip; undertail feathers greyish-yellow; cheeks appear naked and are covered with rows of minute feathers. Female—red patch on brow and back smaller and narrower; noticeably so on belly. Young—little or no red; head green-grey and belly a paler green.

Illiger's Macaw is sometimes mistaken for the Severe Macaw (below) but is easily identified by the red belly patch. It is often kept indoors because it is smaller, usually grows quite tame and is a good imitator. Newly-imported birds must be kept at room temperature and afterwards never at less than 10°C (50°F) wherever possible.

Breeding has sometimes succeeded. A good breeding pair was that at Whipsnade Zoo—one pair reared at least ten youngsters over several years.

During the early days of breeding, the birds enjoyed soaked white bread or rusks, in particular. Other food was the same as that for all Macaws.

Severe Macaw (*A. severa*) Panama, Colombia, Ecuador, Bolivia

Characteristics: 48 cm (19 in) long. Male—green; reddish-brown brow band; edge of wing red; primaries blue; tail feathers reddish-brown with a blue tip; naked-looking cheeks; black beak; iris yellow. Female—reddish-brown brow band less pronounced than male's; rear of head has flattened look. Young— until the age of six months, the iris is black, slowly turning yellow.

The Severe is only half the size of its largest cousins. Its voice is quieter than theirs and it does not possess their strength. The plumage is duller and far less colourful than the other Macaws'. They imitate words very readily and soon grow tame. The Severe Macaw has often been bred. The nest box should be $30 \times 30 \times 70$ cm ($1 \times 1 \times 2$ ft 9 in), with a 10 cm (4 in) deep layer of garden soil mixed with peat, on the bottom; entrance hole diameter 10 cm (4 in); breeding takes place in the flight. The male spends most of his time at the entrance hole but sometimes disappears inside. It spends most of the night inside. A clutch normally contains three to five round white eggs and they are incubated for twenty-four to twenty-six days. The young fly out of the box at about two months. You can tell the sexes immediately because the male has a definite red patch on the brow which the female lacks for the first six months. Hers gradually gets more pronounced.

Occasionally they do not like to be supervised whilst sitting. During breeding they tend to resent the other occupants of the aviary and are inclined to attack them. They do not suffer from the cold.

In the breeding season, offer chopped-up hard-boiled egg, rice, carrots and fruit, sprouting sunflower and oats. They also enjoy leaves.

Scarlet Macaw (*A. macao*) Mexico to Peru (illustrated p. 131)

Characteristics: 85 cm ($33\frac{1}{2}$ in) long. Male—red; wings and shoulders golden-yellow; naked cheeks. Female—smaller; broader and more curved beak. Young—front and middle wing coverts still green; rear wing coverts green with yellow centres; largest, underwing coverts reddish to olive-yellow with obvious red only at the tips.

There are a few breeding pairs in California and Florida. They lay two or three eggs but quite often only one or two youngsters are actually reared, rarely three. The female incubates alone, although the male sometimes sits beside her. In one case the nest box was 60 cm (2 ft) high. It was placed directly on the ground. The youngsters usually emerge from the nest at three months of age. For breeding, they are very keen on bananas, oranges, tomatoes, bread, sunflower, and calcium in various forms.

Green-winged Macaw (*A. chloroptera*) Panama to Paraguay (illustrated p. 131)

Characteristics: 85 cm (33½ in) long. Male—dark red; large upper wing and shoulder coverts olive green; no red feathers in the naked cheeks; upper beak pale with a dark tip; lower beak black. Female—smaller figure and beak.

The Green-wing is also known as the Maroon Macaw. It is known that in the wild they have hybridized with the Military Macaw and with the Blue and Gold Macaw. They have been bred in captivity, where hybridizing is commoner. Wuppertal Zoo hand-reared several youngsters.

Military Macaw (*A. militaris*) Mexico to Argentina (illustrated p. 131)

Characteristics: 65 cm (25½ in) long. Male and female—grass-green; red brow, rump and uppertail coverts blue; underside olive green; four rows of small red feathers on the cheeks; beak black. Young—much duller and more brownish-red; the green edging to the nape is much broader.

This Macaw is named thus because of the dull green of its colouring. It is 20 cm (8 in) smaller than the Large Military Macaw (*A. ambigua*) which has a yellowish-green plumage. Military Macaws are not such good talkers as the other Macaws.

Blue and Gold Macaw (*A. ararauna*) Panama to northern Paraguay

Characteristics: 90 cm (35½ in) long. Male—upper parts blue; lower parts yellow; front of head olive green; a few rows of dark green feathers on the white cheeks. Female—smaller than male, especially the head and beak.

The Blue and Gold is the most intelligent and most lovable of all the Macaws. This makes it very popular and ideally suited to being kept indoors. One breeder actually complained that he could not stand his bird because it was oppressively affectionate! It knew how to get his attention by many methods—swaying body movements, then the most peculiar head posturings, then strange noises. It would do anything to get a human being to notice it and talk to it. They can talk in a high child's voice or in the deeper voice of a grown man. They are said to be capable of remembering some sixty words and phrases.

Blue and Golds have been reared in France for a long time. Magdeburg Zoo bred them in 1965, in an aviary which was only $350 \times 175 \times 240$ cm (11 ft 5 in $\times$ 5 ft 7 in $\times$ 7 ft 9 in). The nest box was $50 \times 50 \times 80$ cm (1 ft 8 in $\times$ 1 ft 8 in $\times$ 2 ft 8 in) with an entrance hole of 17 cm (6¾ in) diameter. It was made of 4 cm (1½ in) thick boards. Every two or three days an egg was laid, usually two or three to a clutch, and incubation lasted about twenty-five days. The beaks of the young were pale, only turning black after six weeks. They left the nest after ten weeks. Their tails were, at most, 20 cm (8 in) long.

They did not reach their final adult length until the age of fifteen months. In Amsterdam Zoo, free-flying Blue and Gold Macaws have bred successfully. They enjoy eating soaked white bread, tomatoes, apples, pears, plums, grapes, oranges, various nuts and sunflower during the breeding season.

Blue Macaws

Hyacinthine Macaw (*Anodorhynchus hyacinthinus*) Brazilian interior (illustrated p. 131)

Characteristics: 95 cm (37½ in) long. Male and female—deep blue; bare eye-ring golden-yellow.

Blue Macaws live along the river courses in the deepest jungle. They are not so shy as the other Macaws but less numerous. Their main food is palm nuts which they devour with ease.

Hyacinthine Macaws live as pairs or in family groups outside the breeding season. They are said to breed in river banks as well. In the zoo at Bratislava (Pressburg) in Czechoslovakia they were reared for the first time and three youngsters were fledged. The nest was in an old wooden box measuring 150 × 150 × 180 cm (5 ft × 5 ft × 6 ft) and there was no flight attached to it. Feeding and rearing as for the other Macaws.

The Hyacinthine Macaw is the largest parrot in the world. It is never found in great numbers in the shops and is more expensive than any other type. There is only one other parrot with a stronger beak. A Blue Macaw can be a most affectionate pet with its owner but quite fierce towards strangers, so beware. It is not one of the gifted talkers.

Conures (*Aratinga*)

Sun Conure/Yellow Conure *A. solstitialis* (4 races)
Petz Conure/Halfmoon Conure *A. canicularis* (3 races)
Golden-crowned Conure *A. aurea* (2 races)

Origin and habit: Central and South America. Since it is the most numerous genus, Conures have the widest distribution of all parrots. Some of them migrate, others are birds of passage. Most species live in the tropical forest, but others live along the river banks in the steppes; a few live in the mountains, up to the tree line. They are very sociable birds, some even staying together as a colony during the breeding season.

They feed on seeds of all types, berries and fruit; some also eat insects. They have been known to do a great deal of damage to crops.

These Conures make their nests in hollow tree tunks, but the occasional few choose holes or rock crevices instead.

General remarks: All these Conures have a wedge-shaped, jagged-edged tail. Several of them are quite beautiful but, unfortunately, they also have very shrill voices. Their behaviour is restless and they tend to use their beaks to destroy anything made of wood. Otherwise, they are hardy and give very little trouble. It is not always possible to house them with other species because they are aggressive and may bite other birds. They are reasonably priced.
Feeding: Canary seed, sunflower, millet, wheat, fruit and berries; fresh green twigs for chewing.

Sun/Yellow Conure (*A. solstitialis solstitialis*) north-west Brazil, Guyana (illustrated p. 132)

Characteristics: 30 cm (12 in) long. Male—sides of head and belly deep orange; breast and back yellow; small primaries have green edges, larger primaries dark blue; broad white eye-ring; beak blackish. Female—narrower white eye-ring; slightly more green in the wings. Young—all yellow plumage variably marked with green; eye-ring blackish.
Housing and rearing: You can only keep these birds indoors when the atmosphere is very moist. They have very loud voices, though a single bird may be quieter.
In the garden: Since 1973/74, a few dealers have offered the Sun Conure for sale. They are amongst the most beautiful of the Conures. Not until the summer do you see the full splendour of their plumage. My own pair made full use of their voices at every conceivable opportunity. The male, particularly, becomes very excited when anyone approaches the nest box. They like a hole to retire into to roost. This species has proved to be a prolific breeder, especially in the USA, where many are hand-reared for sale as pets.

Newly-imported specimens have to be kept at room temperature while they are being acclimatized. Later on, they can stay in the aviary when the temperature drops and will tolerate a few degrees of frost quite happily, as long as they have a box in the shelter, in which to roost.

Jenday Conure (*A. solstitialis jandaya*) east and south-east Brazil

Characteristics: 30 cm (12 in) long. Male—head and throat yellow, ear and eye region sometimes shot through with orange; back green; rump and underparts orange; wings and tail feathers blue; iris grey-brown. Female—less orange on the underparts. Young—greenish with less orange; iris black.
Housing and rearing: Only tame birds can be kept in a metal cage. Imported adult birds are very awkward and have loud voices.
In the garden: The correct housing is a metal construction covered with a very strong wire mesh and with a shelter built of cement or some other hard substance. Because of their beauty, you must forgive their occasional shrieks!

Many have bred successfully and overwintered without heating. They remain as a pair and preen each other happily.

One pair had four eggs, laid in an aviary measuring $3 \times 6 \times 2$ m (9 ft 9 in $\times$ 19 ft 10 in $\times$ 6 ft 6 in). The birds took small twigs in as nesting material, which they broke up into tiny pieces. The male displayed by dancing and bowing before his mate. Sometimes they objected to nest inspection. The male joined the female in the nest box after ten to fourteen days. Whenever he suspected the presence of an intruder, he raised his neck feathers to scare it away. If this failed, both birds retreated into the nest box. Jendays can also be kept flying free. Once a pair have made a nest, accustom each one to free flight in turn. They never go out of calling distance. The young also stay within earshot of their parents.

In the open, the loud voice does not seem so overpowering. This was the case in one small zoo that I visited, where the Jendays were kept at liberty. It is a truly beautiful sight to spot one of these birds in the foliage of a tree.

Petz/Halfmoon Conure (*A. canicularis*) Costa Rica and Mexico

Characteristics: 25 cm ($9\frac{3}{4}$ in) long. Male—green; orange patch on forehead; yellow-orange ring around eye, which has no feathers; pale beak. Female—smaller head and forehead patch.
Housing and rearing. In the house: The small Petz Conure is ideally suited to cage rearing. Young birds soon grow tame and affectionate. They are quite good imitators of words and sounds.
In the garden: Wood is safe, on the whole. Breeding has succeeded several times. Four eggs were laid by one female in a half-open canary nest box and three young were fledged.

Golden-crowned Conure (*A. aurea*) Brazil, Bolivia and Paraguay
(illustrated p. 132)

Characteristics: 28 cm (11 in) long. Male and female—green; forehead and crown orange-yellow; eye region yellowish; iris orange; beak blackish. Young—iris dark brown.
Housing and rearing. In the house: Of all the *Aratinga* Conures, the Golden-crowned is the easiest to keep. It seems to be the most intelligent, learning to imitate words, sneezing, tongue clicking, coughing and whistling. It does not do much wood chewing and has a pleasant voice.

They have bred in a cage. In one case, two or three eggs were laid and incubated for twenty-six days. The nest box measured 20 sq cm and was 27 cm high ($8 \times 8 \times 10\frac{1}{2}$ in). The entrance hole was 5–6 cm ($2-2\frac{1}{4}$ in) diameter. The youngsters left the nest after fifty days. The first brood appeared in April and the second in July. The youngsters were very tame.

In the garden: This species overwinters without heating as long as conditions are frost-free. They have been crossed with Jendays.

Nanday Conures (*Nandayus*)

Nanday Conure (*N. nenday*) (illustrated p. 132)

Characteristics: 31 cm (12¼ in) long. Male—green; head and beak blackish; feet flesh-coloured; thigh feathers red. Female—smaller head; beak more curved. Young—feet blackish.

Origin and habit: South America, from Brazil to Argentina. It is a very common bird in these countries, but is unpopular because of the damage it does to crops and orchards. On the whole, they are shy and cautious.

General remarks: This is a fairly common bird on the market and the price is never very high. A pair stay close together and share all their tasks. They have some very funny habits, such as bobbing up and down, and ruffling their feathers. Chewing and use of voice are both kept within tolerable limits.

Feeding: Sunflower, oats, canary seed, apples, carrots, plums, greenfoods of the usual sort; many like gooseberries and cherries. For breeding, add chopped-up egg mixed with rusks.

Housing and rearing. In the house: Only a tame youngster is suitable for a cage. Old birds are wild and loud. Only all-metal cages are suitable.

In the garden: A flight with shelter attached is very good for these birds. Heating is not required. Breeding has often succeeded. One person had twelve young in one year in his flight measuring 3 × 4 × 2 m (9 ft 9 in × 13 ft × 6 ft 6 in). The nest box was 40 × 40 cm (15¾ × 15¾ in). The female laid four eggs, one every two days. She sat for twenty-five days, the male only entering the box at night. They did not mind nest inspection. The female never left the nest; she just moved over slightly. The parents only protested loudly when strangers, cats or dogs approached them. They are tolerant of finches. They love to bathe and enjoy a shower of rain.

Pyrrhura Conures

White-eared Conure *P. leucotis* (5 races)
Red-bellied Conure *P. frontalis* (3 races)

Origin and habit: Costa Rica and Panama in Central America; South America as far as northern Argentina. The elegant *Pyrrhura* Conures live in the forest-fringed coastal regions, the mountains and in the interior of Brazil. They fly around in flocks of ten to twenty and raid the corn and maize fields, where they cause substantial damage. They nest in hollow branches.

General remarks: They get their name from the reddish-brown colouring, mostly on the underside of the tail. Occasionally one species or another is offered for sale, at a reasonable price. The White-eared Conure is particularly attractive. All *Pyrrhura* need boxes for the night.
Feeding: Sunflower kernels, canary seed, various millets, some hemp, oats, buckwheat, spray millet, fine barley, apples. For breeding, add sprouting spray millet above all, bread and milk, and lettuce.

White-eared Conure (*A. leucotis*) Brazil, Venezuela

Characteristics: 22 cm (8¾ in) long. Male—green; top of head greyish-brown; nape greyish-blue; cheeks reddish-brown; ear region greyish-white; breast grey with white edges to the feathers; shoulder of wing red; central belly area and rump brownish-red; beak black; squarish head. Female—plumage similar to male's but smaller, rounder head. Young—beak grey; duller, washed-out plumage.
Housing and rearing. In the house: Suitable for keeping singly or as a pair in a large cage. They are pleasant, calm little birds which become very tame.
In the garden: White-eared Conures have been bred but only in an aviary. Budgerigars which were housed in the adjoining flight had one or two toes bitten off by them. They get on well with their own kind and you can keep several pairs in one flight. The birds choose their own nesting site—mine chose natural logs fixed beneath the covered portion of the flight. The female gnawed away persistently inside the log until she had furnished for herself a nest hollow 20 cm (8 in) down. This was covered with sawdust and small feathers. She laid four eggs, one every two days, and incubated them for twenty-two days. The male fed her and sometimes spent a few hours by her side during the day. They always spent the night in the box together. At the slightest disturbance, the male fled into the box. They did not like to be observed whilst sitting. Just before the young hatch, the female bathes frequently. This must be a sign that moisture is essential for hatching. The young leave the nest after five weeks and are fed by their parents for a further ten to fourteen days. After two or three months, the plumage of the young-sters is similar to that of their parents. Two broods a year are possible.

Red-bellied Conure (*P. frontalis*) south-east Brazil, Paraguay

Characteristics: 28 cm (11 in) long. Male and female—green; red brow band; ear region and breast faded brown with dark transverse stripes; red belly patch. Young—red brow band and belly patch are less pronounced; head, neck and breast faded yellow.
Housing and rearing. In the house: This slim bird is easily tamed when young. Its voice is unobtrusive and it is capable of imitating a few words. It is possible

to breed them in a cage that is about 1 m (3 ft 3 in) long or in a bird room. *In the garden:* My female laid four eggs in April, which she alone incubated. The male was very aggressive the whole time but did not harm the other residents of the aviary. Both of them fed the young.

They are quite safe in the winter, even when the temperature goes down as low as −22°C (−8°F), because they spend the nights in their boxes.

Caiques (*Pionites*)

Black-headed Caique *P. melanocephala* (2 races)
White-bellied Caique *P. leucogaster* (2 races)

Origin and habit: Venezuela, Guyana, western Brazil, eastern Peru, eastern Ecuador and eastern Colombia. Parrots of this genus rarely come close to human habitation. They live deep in the forest, along the rivers or in the flood plains. After the breeding season, Caiques tend to fly around in loosely associated flocks with no particularly close social structure. Their whistling call resembles that of the tapir. They feed on fruit, berries, buds and nuts.
General remarks: Both these Caiques only occasionally come on to the market. At first they are rather delicate and must be watched carefully. Once acclimatized, however, they are quite durable and hardy, provided that they can roost in a nest box. Try not to choose new imports.
Feeding: Sunflower, all kinds of fruit, various nuts, rusk, biscuits and berries.
Housing and rearing. In the house: These Caiques require warmth and should never be housed cooler than 15°C (59°F). Only very young birds kept alone become tame. If you approach an older bird, watch out for its very powerful beak. They are not good mimics.

Mrs Deurer in Cologne-Deutz has had most success at breeding Caiques. Her Black-headed Caiques had their first two young in 1971. By the end of 1973 there were fifteen of them!

A hybridization of the two species was reported from England. The birds were sensitive to cold and bred in a shelter. The female sat on her four eggs for almost four weeks. All that time, the male attacked anyone who approached. Some ten weeks later, one youngster left the nest. They all shared it at night. In the early days, the youngster ate only germinating seeds, biscuit and nuts. White-bellied Caiques were bred in the USA in 1932. Three young left the nest and grew to independence.

Black-headed Caique (*P. melanocephala*) eastern Venezuela, eastern Peru, eastern Colombia and parts of Guyana

Characteristics: 25 cm (9¾ in) long. Male—wings, back and tail green; black cape; yellow-brown collar; sides of head, throat and legs yellowish; breast and belly whitish; beak and feet blackish; iris red; eye-ring dark. Female—paler eye-rings. Young—the blackish-brown cap feathers have green margins.

General remarks: Black-headed Caiques are very beautiful birds and are popular with fanciers. Some make great use of their powerful voices, others rather less. Since they are small, they do not need large cages, particularly if they can be let out every day.

Feeding: Sunflower, pine cones, apples, berries, cherries and fresh twigs.

Breeding: Black-headed Caiques have bred in a cage measuring 180 cm (6 ft) in length, although they were let out to fly every day. The nest box was 30 cm (1 ft) tall and 20 cm (8 in) wide, with an entrance hole of 6 cm (2¼ in) diameter. The temperature was always 20–24°C (68–75°F). They loved to bathe. Incubation lasted twenty-three days, during which time the male was very aggressive. He only went into the nest at night. The youngsters at first ate only soaked spray millet and figs. After two months, the young left the nest.

White-bellied Caique (*P. leucogaster*) eastern Venezuela, eastern Peru, eastern Colombia and parts of Guyana (illustrated p. 149)

Characteristics: 23 cm (9 in) long. Male and female—wings, back and tail green; cape and nape rust-brown; sides of head, throat and lower belly white-yellow; beak and feet pale flesh colour; iris red.

Housing and rearing: As previous Caique. It has been bred in the USA.

Pionus Parrots

Blue-headed/Red-vented Parrot (*P. menstruus*) (illustrated p. 151)

Characteristics: 27 cm (10½ in) long. Male and female—body and wings predominantly green; head and neck blue; ear region black; undertail coverts red with green tips; beak blackish with red at base of upper beak. Young—beak horny-yellow; head green, sometimes with red frontal band.

Origin and habit: southern Costa Rica, Panama and South America as far as Bolivia. Blue-headed Parrots are sociable, flying around in huge flocks in search of trees that bear ripe fruit. They also raid the maize fields. That is why they are hunted and shot for food. At breeding time they keep to their pairs and usually lay four eggs, in hollow tree trunks. There are eight species in this genus.

General remarks: Most imported birds are still in their juvenile plumage. Their rather plain greenish plumage gives no hint of the colourful splendour which these birds will have when they reach maturity.

In the early days, they are fairly delicate, but once they are acclimatized they become very tame and lovable. They hardly ever learn to talk.

Feeding: Sunflower, canary seed, millet, oats, ground nuts, fruit, greenfood, such as chickweed, lettuce, dandelion and spinach. Young birds must have a good supply of biscuits, rusk, boiled rice or maize and soaked or sprouted sunflower.

Housing and rearing. In the house: I can heartily recommend keeping one young bird because it will become very tame and affectionate. You must maintain room temperature until the bird has acquired its full adult plumage. The voice is soft and rarely heard. It can be kept with other species.

Hawk-headed Parrots (*Deroptyus*)

Guyana Hawk-headed Parrot (*D. accipitrinus*) (illustrated p. 149)

Characteristics: 35 cm (13¾ in) long. Male—front of head whitish; feathers on back of head and nape maroon with broad blue edges; feathers of abdomen and breast also reddish with blue edges; red patch at base of tail; rest of plumage green. Female—smaller form and beak; paler outer eye-ring.

Origin and habit: Northern South America, east Venezuela, Guyana to east Ecuador, northern and parts of southern banks of the Amazon. Another race has a brownish forehead. The Guyana Hawk-head is not common and lives in open tropical woods. It occasionally approaches human habitation. It is not sociable, so is usually only seen singly or in pairs. It breeds in hollow tree trunks, laying up to four eggs.

General remarks: This is the only parrot which can raise a fan on its head. This can be an expression of anger, and is also used to show pleasure and good humour. I was particularly fascinated by the pattern of the breast feathers. When you scratch the head, the bird raises its beautiful nape feathers for you to admire at your leisure. Some specimens are quite happy to come and sit on a finger, being gentle, calm and altogether most lovable. Unfortunately, not many are ever offered for sale and you do not see many in zoos either. Nevertheless, I think it should be mentioned here because it is especially interesting and has some very good characteristics.

Feeding: Sunflower, canary seed, oats, ground nuts, maize, top quality fruit (especially grapes, figs and oranges), rusks soaked in milk, biscuit. Hawk-heads love a varied diet. Give them fresh fruit-tree or willow twigs to chew.

Housing and rearing. In the house: They occasionally let out a loud shriek, particularly if they feel lonely. You will not find it hard to forgive them. They are clever birds and soon become tame. It is very important to their well-being that you let them out of their cages frequently. During the 1970s, several successful breeding attempts were reported in Germany, England and the USA.

In the garden: They can be kept outdoors throughout the year provided that they have a nest box in which to roost.

Amazon Parrots (*Amazona*)

Cuban Amazon *A. leucocephala* (4 races)
San Domingo Amazon *A. ventralis*
Spectacled Amazon *A. albifrons* (3 races)
Green-cheeked Amazon *A. viridigenalis*
Finsch's Amazon *A. finschi*
Yellow-cheeked Amazon *A. autumnalis* (4 races)
Dufresne's Amazon *A. dufresniana* (2 races)
Red-tailed/Blue-faced Amazon *A. brasiliensis*
Festive Amazon *A. festiva* (2 races)
Yellow-shouldered Amazon *A. barbadensis* (2 races)
Blue-fronted Amazon *A. aestiva* (2 races)
Yellow-fronted Amazon *A. ochrocephala* (7 races)
Orange-winged Amazon *A. amazonica* (3 races)
Mealy Amazon *A. farinosa* (4 races)
Vinaceous Amazon *A. vinacea*

Origin and habit: Central and South America, Jamaica, Cuba, the Bahamas, San Domingo, Puerto Rico and the Lesser Antilles. Most species live in the hot temperate zones, some preferring the thickly wooded regions and others more open habitats. They are mainly found, however, in the lowland woodlands, coasts and swamps. On the ground they are rather clumsy, but they are excellent climbers.

Outside the breeding season, you find them pursuing all their activities in flocks. They have their own roosts, flying off in the morning to search for food and returning each to his own place for the night, all the while making a tremendous noise. They stay in pairs throughout. Whilst feeding they keep perfectly still, so quiet that you can actually hear the shells and rinds of the fruits and berries as they fall to the ground. Their natural breeding time is during our winter. They nest in hollow tree trunks in the forests.

General remarks: Imported Amazons have been caught in the wild. Occasionally, the odd tame or half-tame bird will arrive, generally one which was caught when very young. In their early days in captivity, they are noisy and raise their nape feathers. Young birds calm down sooner than older ones.

Amazons are now the commonest large psittacines in captivity. They are popular pets and if obtained when young, they will grow tame quickly and learn to talk. Since no one has yet established that Amazons are born talkers, it is pure luck if you get a good talker. Some have learnt up to 100 words, as well as whistling, singing and other sounds, but everything they say sounds parrot-like. Most Amazons are not as good at imitating the tone of the human voice as African Greys. Amazons never lose their natural voices completely and usually lapse into them when they are bored. Most tame Amazons have a

145

more affectionate temperament than African Greys. Amazons are never malicious or deceitful, and always grateful for human company. Some species are more intelligent than others—details are given below.

There is still some confusion over naming the various species. One species can have three or four names and a researcher can easily become confused. It is always wise to check by asking for the scientific name, because prices vary enormously from species to species. Other complications arise between races, and also in regard to the adult plumage. It can take years for a youngster to acquire its adult plumage. Young birds have a black or dark brown iris, which turns yellow or orange later.

Never hurry your decision about the purchase of an Amazon. The bird you choose will become one of the family, a real character; and your family must get used to their feathered friend, and he to them. For this reason, an Amazon should never be bought on impulse; it is something that you must all give a great deal of thought to beforehand.

Feeding: Large sunflower, boiled maize, oats, wheat, some hemp and canary seed, walnuts, ground nuts and hazel nuts. Good sweet fruit—apples, pears, bananas, oranges, cherries, peaches; and various berries—blackcurrants, gooseberries, strawberries, bilberries, raspberries and rowan berries. Also, peas, sometimes with their pods, bread and milk, fresh fruit, poplar, willow or elder twigs for chewing. Young, newly-imported birds should be fed fresh corn on the cob or maize (boiled until soft), boiled rice, sprouting sunflower seeds and fruit. Gradually accustom them to hard foods later.

Housing and rearing. In the house: Cages of 50–70 cm (1 ft 8 in–2 ft 9 in) length are used for Amazons. This size is also appropriate for African Greys. They must be stout metal constructions with very good fastenings and thick, strong feeders. I do not recommend round or white cages because all that the bird inside can see is a curved surface. Some people believe that every birdcage that comes on to the market must be perfect. Unfortunately, cages are sometimes designed by theoreticians and aesthetes, and turn out to be thoroughly impractical. It is particularly important that Amazons, whose droppings are softer and moister than those of the seed-eaters, have a cage which is easily kept clean, because cleanliness is the first rule.

Amazons can also be kept on a stand. The perch must be about 60 cm (2 ft) long and made of wood, never metal. Make it easy to remove for cleaning. Each end of the perch should house a feeder which you can remove easily— but do not make it so easy that your parrot can get it out, too! If the stand can incorporate an additional branch, for climbing, so much the better. There should be a platform underneath the stand, some 60–70 cm (2 ft–2 ft 9 in) long by 50–60 cm (1 ft 8 in–2 ft) across, which is strewn with sand. This is to catch droppings and food remnants.

You must always supervise a bird, when training it to use a stand; at night, the bird should be put back into its cage. This is the routine you should aim for. It will always be easier to achieve with a young bird; older birds can be obstinate and spend hours squawking with fear as soon as anyone tries to approach them. You can tell a youngster by the flecks in the beak, the black or brown eyes and the incomplete plumage coloration.

Many Amazons never entirely give up making parrot noises, particularly if they are bored or do not get much attention. Putting other parrots in the room with them to keep them company only encourages such noises.

The difficulty in sexing Amazons is one of the major obstacles in breeding these birds.

The best place to try breeding them would be an attic, a small room or an indoor flight. You would have to use very stout wire netting and avoid wood because many Amazons love chewing it.

The best chances of success come when you are able to put several pairs in together and wait for them to form their own breeding pairs. You then remove the superfluous birds. Hollow tree trunks or thickly walled barrels can be installed for this purpose. If you want to build your own nest box, you must use very stout hardwood timbers. The entrance hole should be between 10 and 15 cm (4–6 in), depending on the species. Use thick hardwood branches or a climbing tree for the bird to climb on.

In the garden: If you clip one wing of a tame Amazon it can be left out in the garden in the summer. A once-weekly shower of warm rain will do no harm; in fact, it is necessary. If it does not rain, you have to spray the bird yourself, using warm water in a plant spray. Acclimatized Amazons can be kept outdoors all year round but newly-imported specimens should be maintained at room temperature.

Cuban Amazon (*A. leucocephala*) Cuba, the Bahamas and the Cayman Islands (illustrated p. 152)

Characteristics: 31 cm (12¼ in) long. Male and female—green; black edging to feathers; forehead white; cheeks and throat red; centre of belly wine-red; beak yellow-white. Young—no white on top of head; cheeks green with a few red feathers.

This species is becoming rarer in the wild because of man's encroachments on its forest habitat. There, they live on fruit and berries. Between April and July, three or four eggs are laid in hollow palm trees.

Newly-imported birds are rather delicate at first, but once they have acclimatized they become quite hardy. They have gentle, even temperaments and are highly praised for their intelligence. Their repetition of words is not always the clearest, but there is no doubt about their beauty. One attempt to cross a male Cuban with a female Blue-fronted Amazon succeeded; three eggs hatched but only one youngster survived. In 1909, an English breeder had three eggs from his *A. l. bahamensis*. One hatched, but the bird died soon after. One successful attempt was reported from the GDR in 1975. One youngster survived.

San Domingo/Hispaniolan/Sallés Amazon (*A. ventralis*) San Domingo (illustrated p. 152)

Characteristics: 30 cm (12 in) long. Male—green; black-edged feathers; white forehead and eye-ring; crown and cheeks dark blue; black ear patches; centre of belly reddish; beak yellow-white; primaries and secondaries blue. Female—smaller head and beak; narrower white eye-ring.

Very little is known about this bird to date. I once kept this rare Amazon. They are very delicate at first, but gradually accustom themselves to room temperature. They are very vital, lively and amusing birds. My pair would hang from the ceiling, fool around and take titbits from each other's beaks. They love fresh twigs, especially if they have berries, like rose hips and rowans. Their only drawback is that they make great use of their very powerful voices.

Spectacled Amazon (*A. albifrons*) Guatemala, Mexico, Honduras, Nicaragua, Costa Rica (illustrated p. 152)

Characteristics: 27 cm (10¼ in) long. Male—green; dark-edged feathers; forehead white; crown blue; scarlet eye region; beak yellow; red patch on primaries and alula; iris orange. Female—primaries and alula are green. Young—iris brown.

The Spectacled Amazon is so called because of the broad red ring round the eyes. They are frequently kept as caged pets in their homeland, and are said to be good talkers. They were bred in America in 1949.

Page 149
Top left: White-bellied Caique (*Pionites leucogaster*)
Top right: Guyana Hawk-headed Parrot (*Deroptyus accipitrinus*)
Bottom left: North Moluccan Eclectus Parrot (*Lorius roratus vosmaeri*)
Bottom right: Yellow-bellied Senegal Parrot (*Poicephalus senegalus*)

Page 150
Top left: Derbyan (*Psittacula derbyana*)
Top right: African Ringneck Parrakeet (*Psittacula krameri*)
Bottom left: Alexandrine Parrakeet (*Psittacula eupatria*)
Bottom right: Moustache Parrakeet (*Psittacula alexandri*)

Page 151
Top: A pair of Plum-head Parrakeets (*Psittacula cyanocephala*)
Bottom: Blue-headed Parrot (*Pionus menstruus*)

Green-cheeked Amazon (*A. viridigenalis*) north-east Mexico (illustrated p. 152)

Characteristics: 43 cm (17 in) long. Male and female—green; top of head red; back feathers have dark edging; on either side of the eyes, a blue band stretches up the sides of the head; primaries have dark blue tips; red wing coverts; tail feathers green only; beak pale; iris yellow-brown. Young—only the forehead is red.

Because of the red crown, this species is also sometimes known as the Mexican Red-head. It is very similar to the Finsch's Amazon. Two of these Amazons were imported to Germany in 1878 by Miss Hagenbeck for the first time ever. Many of them become very good talkers. When excited they raise the neck feathers to form a sort of ruff.

Hybridizing with a Spectacled Amazon succeeded in 1934. Four youngsters hatched and three survived.

Finsch's Amazon (*A. finschi*) Mexico (illustrated p. 152)

Characteristics: 32 cm (12½ in) long. Male and female—green; forehead and lores dark red; top and rear of head blue; feathers of underside of body have black edging; no red in the tail feathers; beak horn coloured.

This species is named after the man who first described it. In recent years, it has been imported in greater numbers, but often it is not recognized for what it is. This is another of the Amazons that have bred in California.

Yellow-cheeked Amazon (*A. autumnalis autumnalis*) Mexico, Guatemala, Honduras, Nicaragua, Costa Rica, Colombia, Ecuador and north-west Brazil (illustrated p. 152)

Characteristics: 35 cm (13¾ in) long. Male and female—green; nape feathers have a blackish edging; brow and lores red; crown pale blue; yellowish beneath the eyes; red tint in the smaller primaries; beak horn-grey. Talking is

1 Cuban Amazon (*A. leucocephala*); 2 San Domingo Amazon (*A. ventralis*); 3 Spectacled Amazon (*A. albifrons*); 4 Green-cheeked Amazon (*A. viridigenalis*); 5 Finsch's Amazon (*A. finschi*); 6 Yellow-cheeked Amazon (*A. autumnalis/*; 7 Dufresne's Amazon (*A. defresniana*); 8 Red-tailed/Blue-faced Amazon (*A. brasiliensis*); 9 Festive Amazon (*A. f. festiva*); 10 Bodin's Amazon (*A. f. bodini*); 11 Yellow-shouldered Amazon (*A. barbadensis*); 12 Blue-fronted Amazon (*A. ae. aestiva*); 13 Yellow-fronted Amazon (*A. o. ochrocephala*); 14 Panama Amazon (*A. o. panamensis*); 15 Yellow-naped Amazon (*A. o. auropalliata*); 16 Mexican Double-yellow Head (*A. o. oratrix*); 17 Orange-winged Amazon (*A. amazonica*); 18 Vinaceous Amazon (*A. vinacea*)

not their primary accomplishment. Once fully coloured, however, the Yellow-cheeked is the most beautiful of the Amazons.

Diademed Amazon (*A. autumnalis diadema*) north-west Brazil

Characteristics: A race of the Yellow-cheeked, the Diademed Amazon has a lilac-coloured scalp; the back of the head is greenish-yellow; nape feathers are green with lilac tips.

Dufresne's Amazon (*A. dufresniana*) Guyana, south-east Brazil (illustrated p. 152)

Characteristics: 36 cm (14 in) long. Male and female—green; forehead and lores orange-yellow; cheek and throat feathers have blue tips; the first four primaries form an orange speculum; the four feathers on the inside edges of the tail are orange-yellow; upper beak dark horn except for the root, which is reddish. Young—green head without red; orange wing coverts; tail green.

Also known as the Granada Amazon, the Dufresne's Amazon is very rarely offered for sale. Some people maintain that it is an intelligent and gifted talker; others say that it has none of these talents. *A. d. rhodocorytha*, the Red-browed Amazon, came into Europe in small numbers in 1975. Young birds have been known to become very tame. Sometimes the voice can be extremely loud. Export has now been forbidden.

Red-tailed/Blue-faced Amazon (*A. brasiliensis*) southern Brazil (illustrated p. 152)

Characteristics: 36 cm (14 in) long. Male and female—green; forehead, lores, wing edges and bases of tail feathers red; crown yellow; sides of head violet; beak horny brown. Very rarely exported.

Festive Amazon (*A. festiva festiva*) eastern Ecuador and Peru (illustrated p. 152)

Characteristics: 35 cm (13¾ in) long. Male and female—lores and edge of brow red; temples, eyebrows and chin-patch blue; back and rump red; beak flesh coloured; no wing speculum.

You do not often find one of these on the market, but they are not yet rare. Some of them are very clear talkers.

There have also been yellow versions of the Festive Amazon, although there is some speculation that they were in fact Lutinos that happened to have red eyes and pale feet. It is said that the natives of South America know how to apply the secretions of a certain poisonous frog to the feathers of this bird in order to turn them yellow.

154

Bodin's Amazon (*A. festiva bodini*) Venezuela and north-west Guyana (illustrated p. 152)

Characteristics: 34 cm (13¼ in) long. Male and female—green but with yellowish-green underparts; red extends as far as the crown; lower back and rump red; bluish cheeks; black stripe on lores; blackish beak.

Yellow-shouldered Amazon (*A. barbadensis*) Venezuela and off-shore islands (illustrated p. 152)

Characteristics: 34 cm (13¼ in) long. Male—brow, temples, chin and cheeks yellow; bend of wing yellow; wing coverts red; beak grey-white. Female—said to be blue-green on the breast and belly.

There are several alternative names for this Amazon: Yellow-winged Amazon and Little Yellow-headed Amazon. It is best to avoid these names, to reduce confusion with other species. The distinguishing feature is the broad yellow shoulder, which gives it its proper name.

Yellow-shouldered Amazons grow very tame and become good talkers, which makes them good indoor subjects. Some were bred in 1974.

Blue-fronted Amazon (*A. aestiva aestiva*) Brazil, Bolivia, Paraguay and northern Argentina (illustrated p. 152)

Characteristics: 36–38 cm (14–15 in) long. Male and female—green; pale blue forehead; crown, cheeks and throat yellow; bend of wing red or yellow (on upper wing edge only); wing coverts red, beak blackish, iris orange. Young—head washed-out greenish-blue-yellow; much paler colour to bend of wing, iris black.

The Blue-front is one of the most readily available Amazons on the market. Sometimes it is called the Red-shouldered Amazon, but this is misleading since one of its races, *A. aestiva xanthopteryx*, has a yellow bend of wing with a narrow edging of red. The blues and yellows of this Amazon vary greatly, depending on age.

This Amazon is always praised for its tameness and imitative skill. Some birds even learn to imitate dogs and to sing. They copy cats and many other everyday noises. One Blue-front is said to have reached the ripe old age of 117 years. Breeding and hybridizing have been successful many times. One Scottish breeder reared two young in a cage measuring 60 × 60 × 30 cm (2 × 2 × 1 ft). In the first year, the brood appeared in May; the second year, in June. Blue-fronted Amazons have also bred in an aviary.

As a rule, the female lays three to five eggs which she incubates for twenty-eight days, all the time being fed by her mate. Their favourite nesting site is the hollow of an old log, preferably not a very deep one. The diameter of the entrance should be about 12–14 cm (4¾–5½ in).

The young leave the nest after about sixty days and are fed by their parents for a long time afterwards. You must also offer them plenty of fruit, berries, partially ripe corn, germinating sunflower and, sometimes, pheasant food.

Amazons are also kept flying free.

Mutations: There have been reports of pale blue, pied yellow and Lutino Blue-fronted Amazons.

Yellow-fronted Amazon (*A. ochrocephala*) Colombia, Venezuela, Guyana, Surinam, Ecuador, Peru, Panama, Costa Rica, the Honduras and Mexico

Characteristics: 36–43 cm (14–17 in) long. Male and female—green; front or whole head yellow; red wing coverts; bend of wing and edge of wing yellow to red; beak blackish or whitish.

This species has the most races, so there are great colour variations. For this reason, I shall mention the most common ones individually.

Surinam Yellow-fronted Amazon (*A. ochrocephala ochrocephala*) Colombia, Venezuela, Guyana and Surinam (illustrated p. 152)

Characteristics: 40 cm (15¾ in) long. Male and female—green; underparts yellowish with narrow blackish edging to the feathers; front of head yellow with a few green feathers in the brow; bend of wing and coverts red; beak reddish at the base and blackish at the tip. Young—front of head duller and less yellow; little red in the bend of wing and coverts.

Sometimes this race is called the Single Yellow-head Amazon. They can become very tame and are very skilful imitators. Some birds will let you lay them on their backs and tickle them. They learn to speak several words, as well as imitating miaouing, barking, coughing, sneezing and whistling.

Panama Amazon (*A. ochrocephala panamensis*) Panama and northern Colombia (illustrated p. 152)

Characteristics: 36 cm (14 in) long. Male and female—distinguished from the previous race by the yellowish lower beak; also have pale yellow forehead; no blackish edging to feathers on upper body; overall appearance of dark blue-green.

This is another intelligent and lovable race. Recently, more are being imported. One youngster was reared in the USA in 1945.

Yellow-naped Amazon (*A. ochrocephala auropalliata*) western Mexico, north-west Costa Rica and northern Honduras (illustrated p. 152)

Characteristics: 37–39 cm (14½–15¼ in) long. Male and female—green head;

yellow patch on nape; occasionally a few yellow feathers in the forehead; bend of wing and coverts red; beak dark horn grey. Young—said to lack yellow nape patch.

This is one of the less commonly imported species. It is one of the most talented of all mimics. It is said to have been bred in England and overseas.

Mexican Double Yellow-head (*A. ochrocephala oratrix*) Mexico and British Honduras (illustrated p. 152)

Characteristics: 39–43 cm (15¼–17 in) long. Male—green; feathers have small dark edges; whole head yellow; legs yellow; bend of wing and coverts red; edge of wing yellow; beak yellowish-white. Female—smaller with shorter, broader beak. Young—head almost completely green at first; forehead, crown and sides of head gradually turn yellow. Coloration takes four years.

Sometimes known as the Greater Yellow-head or just Yellow-head, this is one of the largest, most beautiful and most sought-after Amazons. Young birds grow very tame, older birds are more difficult. They are intelligent and quick to learn, and can repeat words, noises, songs and whole sentences in a thoroughly true-to-life voice.

Unfortunately, you rarely find these birds for sale, and this, together with their talents, makes them very expensive. Mexican Double Yellow-heads are said to have hatched young in America in 1944, and in England in 1970.

Orange-winged Amazon (*A. amazonica*) Colombia, Venezuela, Guyana, eastern Brazil, eastern Ecuador, north-east Peru and Surinam (illustrated p. 152)

Characteristics: 33 cm (13 in) long. Male and female—green; eyebrow stripe, forehead and lores blue; crown, cheeks and base of primaries yellow; wing coverts red; beak yellow-brown.

Many call this the Venezuelan Amazon; it is also often confused with the Blue-fronted Amazon. The Orange-wing always has a green bend of wing, the Blue-fronted a red one. The former's beak is yellow-brown, the latter's blackish. The bluish-yellow colouring varies greatly, so this cannot be any indication of species.

Young Orange-wings can become very tame; older birds, however, almost always remain wild and noisy.

Mealy Amazon (*A. farinosa*) eastern Venezuela, Guyana, Surinam, Peru, Panama; also, north-west South America as far as Ecuador, Nicaragua, Costa Rica, Mexico, Honduras and Guatemala.

Characteristics: 40 cm (15¾ in) long. Male and female—green; black edging to nape feathers; back sprinkled with grey; sometimes crown is orange-violet;

157

wing coverts red; narrow red border to wings; upper mandible flesh-coloured base, blackish towards the tip; lower beak blackish.

The Mealy Amazon is so-called because of the powdery effect of the grey feathers on the back. It is one of the best talkers, but some never completely give up screeching. Others remain virtually silent. Mealy Amazons are not often offered for sale, so the price is usually quite high. They do not need heating in winter.

Vinaceous Amazon (*A. vinacea*) south-east Brazil and Paraguay (illustrated p. 152)

Characteristics: 36 cm (14 in) long. Male—green; black-edged feathers; lores and beak red; upper throat and breast burgundy-red; nape feathers bluish; iris orange. Female darker tinge and less red in beak. Young—lores pale red; underparts duller with broad green edges to feathers; beak red at base only; iris yellow.

Export of this species is now forbidden. They have a calm and gentle temperament but are not good talkers. Olders specimens rarely become tame.

Poicephalus Parrots

Yellow-bellied Senegal Parrot (*P. senegalus*, 3 races) (illustrated p. 149)

Characteristics: 24 cm (9½ in) long. Male—green; head dark grey; breast and belly yellow to orange; iris yellow. Female—duller plumage; head grey; underbelly, rump and undertail coverts yellow with green feathers scattered throughout. Young—black iris; cap very dark grey; ash-grey cheeks. Iris changes colour during the second year.
Origin and habit: West Africa, from Senegal to the Cameroons. Three races of Senegal Parrots live in west Africa, north of the equator. The most beautiful is the orange-bellied Senegal Parrot *P. s. versteri*, which has a brilliant orange underbelly. They are very common in their homeland. They cause extensive damage to the banana and maize plantations.
General remarks: The Yellow-bellied Senegal Parrot is the only race that is continuously on sale and always at a reasonable price. Contrary to previous belief, the shading on the underside from yellow to orange has nothing to do with the sex of the bird, it is a racial difference. Young birds can become very tame and affectionate and give much pleasure, but birds caught when older often remain wild and aggressive. They are usually timid. Young birds will learn to talk, though not always clearly. Some are better at whistling.
Feeding: Sunflower, oats, various nuts, berries, corn on the cob or maize, wheat, apples and roots. For breeding, feed mainly apples and carrots, nuts and sprouting sunflower, oats and wheat. Not all like soft foods.

Young Yellow-bellied Senegal
Parrots can become very tame.

Housing and rearing. In the house: A typical parrot cage with strong metal bars
is essential because these birds have very strong beaks. I recommend the use
of a thick branch of oak or beech for a perch. Since you can only really tame a
young bird, look for one with dark eyes, because the iris does not change to
yellow until the age of twelve months.

Several years ago, a Danish man succeeded in rearing some youngsters in
a cage measuring $44 \times 44 \times 60$ cm high (1 ft $5\frac{1}{4}$ in $\times$ 1 ft $5\frac{1}{4}$ in $\times$ 2 ft) the nest
box on the outside of the cage. This measured 25×25 cm ($9\frac{3}{4} \times 9\frac{3}{4}$ in) and
was 35 cm (1 ft $1\frac{3}{4}$ in) high. Three or four eggs were laid. The brood months
were January and March.

In the garden: Naturally, it will be easier to breed them in a flight with an
attached shelter. The main difficulty is in trying to sex the birds. This is
complicated by age and race factors. Quite often, you can only make your
decision after observing the behaviour of the birds. One breeding success
occurred in 1957 in England. Three youngsters were reared. The nest box
was 25×25 cm ($9\frac{3}{4} \times 9\frac{3}{4}$ in) and 60 cm (2 ft) high. It was hung under the roof
of the flight and so was exposed to the outside temperature. Senegal Parrots
were also bred in Leipzig in 1967. This flight measured $2 \times 1 \times 2$ m (6 ft

6 in × 3 ft 3 in × 6 ft 6 in). The birds refused to use a natural log, a block of oak measuring 2 m (6 ft 6 in) in length with a hollow measuring 35 cm (1 ft 1¾ in). Instead, they chose to return to an old site they had constructed themselves. This was 25 cm (9¾ in) broad, 20 cm (8 in) deep and 40 cm (1 ft 3¾ in) high. They gnawed a second entrance hole into it and used the pieces of wood this provided as a nest lining. The male's display consisted of a dance with his wings spread out, fan-like, and the nape feathers raised like a ruff. All the time, strange mating calls could be heard. Three eggs were laid in the March, and the female incubated them for twenty-two days, guarded at the entrance by the male. Eleven weeks later a youngster in full plumage left the nest. It was paler and smaller than its parents. Its underbelly had only a hint of yellow. The overwintering temperature was 10°–12°C (50°–54°F); at breeding time it was never lower than 15°C (59°F), 28°C (82°F) by day. F. J. Weber in Kirchen has had many successes in breeding this species since 1970. As to building the aviary, I ought also to add that you should never use wood and always use very stout wire netting because these birds have very strong beaks and can destroy all sorts of things. I have known some pull out staples without the slightest effort.

Meyer's Parrot (*P. meyeri*) Eritrea, Uganda, Kenya, Tanzania, Mozambique, Zambia, Angola, Botswana and northern Zimbabwe

Characteristics: 22 cm (8¾) long. Male and female—olive brown; hint of yellow in crown; bend of wing, underwing and thigh yellow; breast, belly and undertail coverts bluish-green; beak and legs blackish; iris red. Young—no yellow in the thigh; little yellow in the shoulders.
General remarks: Six to eight races of this species are known across the whole of this vast area. The colour differentiations are mainly on the belly, and the rump shows more or less blue or blue-green. There are also some races which show no yellow in the shoulder. Their size and figure betray a close relationship to the Senegal Parrot. Since the 1970s, they have been more frequently imported. Older specimens remain shy, though younger ones eventually grow more trusting. No one knows if they are good imitators. Once they have become acclimatized they can be overwintered in cool conditions. Avoid frost, however. They are tolerant of their own kind, so they may also tolerate other species.
Feeding: As for Senegal Parrot.
Breeding: A few breeders have reported successes recently, above all in Sweden and England. H. Hülso in Bevergern reared three youngsters in 1975, the first of which did not emerge from the nest until twelve weeks after hatching. The breeding took place in one of the larger aviaries. On the whole, three to four eggs will be laid. There are no known plumage indications of the sex of an adult bird.

160

African Grey Parrot (*Psittacus*)

African Grey Parrot (*P. erithacus*, 2 races) Africa—Ivory Coast to the
Congo, Principe Island and Fernando Poó (illustrated below)

Characteristics: Around 36 cm (14 in) long. Male—grey; naked face; black
beak; tail red; iris watery-yellow to corn yellow. Female—smaller head, beak
and body than male; underside often paler. Young—iris at first black, several
months later it is dark grey to pale grey, then becomes watery-yellow to corn
yellow. The time this takes varies.

Timneh Parrot (*P. erithacus timneh*) Guinea, Sierra Leone, Liberia and
western parts of the Ivory Coast.

Characteristics: Around 32 cm (12½ in) long. Male and female—dark grey;
reddish-brown tail feathers; upper beak horn to flesh coloured at the base,
black-grey at the tip and on the lower mandible.

Breeding pair of African Greys: *left*, female; *right*, male.

Origin and habit: Western woodland areas of Guinea, Sierra Leone, Liberia, Ivory Coast, Congo and Angola. The two races of African Greys live north and south of the equator. The pale grey birds come from the southern parts and the rarer dark ones from the north.

Once breeding is over, they go around in huge flocks. They each have their own particular sleeping place in the tallest trees, and taking off in the morning to search for food is a noisy business. They eat fruit and maize, large seeds and berries. Their main enemy is man.

General remarks: In earlier times, many African Greys did not survive the lengthy voyage to Europe. Nowadays, however, they arrive in good condition. Some will have a black or grey iris, a sign that they are young birds, and these will be the easiest to tame. Birds with yellow eyes are older and far more difficult. However, the latter are hardier, but many never trust human beings completely. The temper of a bird is always betrayed by its pupils and nape feathers. The pupils oscillate, from large to small, indicating that the bird is highly agitated, and the owner had better watch out! Likewise, the raising of the nape feathers bodes no good, so guard your fingers well! Such unevenness of temper is a drawback of many African Greys. If you are lucky enough to acquire a very young bird, or even one that has been fussed over all its short life, you will find that it turns into a very lovable and tame pet. However, one sudden burst of temper could ruin your bird for life.

Without a doubt, the African Grey is the king of the imitators. It is not just that they can faithfully reproduce a human voice down to the smallest detail of intonation; they also know when to use appropriate phrases. At night, for instance, they know that only 'Goodnight!' is appropriate; in the morning, it's 'Good morning!', and so on. They are also able to fit the right words to a given situation. For example, the phone rings; immediately the parrot responds, 'Hello! Oldenburg here', in precisely the tone of voice that you normally use. They can faithfully imitate the following, amongst many others: master calling dog by name, drawing of a cork, sneezing, laughing or coughing, whistling a tune, a creaking door, pouring wine; in fact, nothing is too difficult for them. There is no other parrot which approaches their skill.

Once domesticated they usually give up making parrot noises completely. You seldom hear piercing shrieks from them. A change of position, or owner, will be greeted with a long silence by the African Grey.

Of course, this capacity for imitation varies from bird to bird. On the whole, women's or children's voices are more faithfully reproduced than men's. Size, colour, race and sex have nothing at all to do with intelligence. Sometimes it is many months before a Grey repeats a word. Gentle, reliable treatment is the key. Moving the cage or changing any other circumstances will not help at all, nor will anything be gained by yelling at your bird.

Feeding: Sunflower, peanuts and other nuts, rusks, fruit, greenfood (spinach, lettuce, dandelion, chickweed), branches from pines, willows or limes for chewing. Also, additional protein in the form of cubes of cheese, boiled bones or lean chicken or veal. Never feed raw meat as this could lead to the bird becoming a feather plucker.

Young birds (with a black iris) should be fed soaked rusk with scrambled egg and boiled rice, soaked spray millet or some other sprouting seed.

Housing and rearing. In the house: The cage should not be made of copper or brass because of verdigris, and the cleaning fluid you have to use can be just as harmful. I do not recommend small round cages, nor square cages. The most suitable is usually a rectangular cage with a very good door fastening, and fixed feeders made of porcelain. The cage should not be next to a heater nor in constant summer sun. On the contrary, the morning and evening sun suits the birds best. They are also refreshed by a shower once or twice weekly, or by a warm shower of rain in the summer. For the first two or three weeks, leave your newcomer in peace. Give him time to adjust. If you want your Grey to develop into a tame talker, it has to be the only bird in the room.

African Greys are as long lived as many humans. One bird died at the age of seventy-three, simply of old age.

In the garden: African Greys are kept in flights only for breeding. Several successes have been reported in recent years. It is assumed that they are not sexually mature until the age of five, although they do pair up after the age of about two. This means, of course, that you may have a very long wait ahead of you, especially as the pair may not be compatible. Someone who can afford to buy several birds at once stands a much better chance of success, because he can leave the choice of mate to the birds.

It is not always easy to tell the sexes apart; however, it is only the female which gives a rather sharp, clear call, something like 'pink'.

The aviary should be constructed of iron or steel poles covered with stout netting, and must contain a shelter for the birds to spend the winter in. Anything less than $-3°C$ (27°F) can harm the feet. The nest box should have thick walls and be about 35×35 cm (1 ft $1\frac{3}{4} \times 1$ ft $1\frac{3}{4}$ in) and 60 cm (2 ft) deep. The entrance hole diameter should be 12 cm ($4\frac{3}{4}$ in). The feeders should be high up.

The mating display consists of the male dancing round his chosen female with his wings drooping. He feeds her. Breeding in Europe starts in the summer or autumn. Two to four eggs are laid. The female sits for about thirty days and is fed frequently through the entrance by the male. She spends most of her time keeping the youngsters warm. Later on, the male helps with the feeding in the nest box. The young appear flesh-coloured and have pale feet and beaks. They leave the nest around ten weeks of age.

Whenever you approach the aviary, the African Grey will fluff up its feathers, turning itself into a ball, as a means of frightening you off (just as owls do). If anything untoward happens, the young fly back into the nestbox in a flash. They are fed by their parents intermittently for about four months.

Pairing dances and feeding of the female have been observed in two-year-olds, but not until they were six years old did they lay four eggs and rear their young.

At breeding time give them plenty of chickweed and dandelion, soaked white bread with added sucrose, plenty of seedlings, boiled rice, rice in the husks and peas.

Psittacula Parrakeets

Alexandrine Parrakeet *P. eupatria* (5 races)
African Ringneck Parrakeet *P. krameri* (6 races)
Moustache Parrakeet *P. alexandri* (7 races)
Derbyan *P. derbyana*
Plum-head/Blossom-headed Parrakeet *P. cyanocephala* (2 races)

Origin and habit: India and countries to the east; Africa. After breeding, these Parrakeets are seen flying about in huge flocks. If they are left alone, they become bold and confident. They are extremely good fliers and very skilful climbers, but on the ground they are very clumsy. In some parts of India they are a protected species. They evade capture astutely, disappearing high up into the trees where they can no longer be spotted, because of their green plumage. Outside the breeding season they roost in huge flocks high up in the trees. They prefer damp hilly areas that are thickly wooded and the lower stretches of rivers. They are found at altitudes of up to 3500 metre.

They live on fruit and seeds of all kinds. They also raid plantations of corn, rice, maize and fruit.

Although they are tree-dwellers, they also build their nests in cliffs and walls, and even in niches in the pagodas. In India, the main breeding season is between November and March.

General remarks: Birds of this genus are among man's oldest friends. The Romans would pay more for a talking Parrakeet than they would for a slave. Alexandrines and Indian Ringnecks are always available. Some species are imported in large numbers and are offered at a reasonable price. These birds have always been caught in the wild, and there is a high proportion of youngsters among them. If they are still in their juvenile plumage, it is difficult to sex them. Often, you have to wait until they are two years old. Many take until their third year to achieve full adult plumage.

Feeding: Sunflower, oats, wheat, canary seed, some hemp, millet, apple, rusk and greenfood. For larger types, add small nuts, fresh maize, rice, and fresh twigs for chewing.

Housing and rearing. In the house: When kept singly in a cage, young ones become very tame and are able to learn all sorts of skills. They repeat words and whistle tunes very well. Males are more gifted than females. Old birds cannot be tamed; they bite and are very wilful.

The larger species have very powerful voices, but the Plum-head Parrakeet does not, which makes it suitable for rearing in the house.

In the garden: The larger types are only suitable for breeding in an aviary, which must be constructed of stout wire netting on an iron or steel frame and contain a shelter built out of some hard material to withstand the attacks of the extremely powerful beaks which these birds possess. The flight should be 2–4 m (6 ft 6 in–13 ft) in length, depending on the size of the birds. The nest box must also be of stout, thick wood. Breeding has succeeded so well with some species that there have even been mutations, and very beautiful they are.

Once they have acclimatized, they can be overwintered without heating. Protect them from more than one or two degrees of frost, however, otherwise they might suffer frost-bitten feet. It is best to keep them in a well-insulated shelter in winter. No species, except the Plum-head, should be kept with other birds because they are liable to bite off the toes of weaker birds.

Alexandrine Parrakeet (*P. eupatria*) India, Sri Lanka, Burma and Kampuchea (illustrated p. 150)

Characteristics: 45 cm (17¾ in) long. Male—green; neckband is pink at the nape and black at the sides; brown-red patch on the shoulders; beak red. Female—no neckband. Young—as female; at around eighteen months brown shoulder patches appear; full adult plumage at about three years.

Housing and rearing: The Alexandrine Parrakeet breeds as early as February or March. The male's display consists of leaping and bowing before the chosen female with his wings spread out. He then feeds her. The nest box needs a base of about 30 × 30 cm (1 × 1 ft) and needs to be about 60 cm (2 ft) deep. The entrance hole diameter should be 8–9 cm (3–3½ in). The females are inclined to suffer from egg-binding, because they lay in the colder weather. The three to five eggs are laid on a base of wood shavings, peat or sawdust. They prefer nest boxes outside to ones in the shelter.

Rearing foods should consist of oats, wheat, corn on the cob, berries and fruit. They are sexually mature at two, but their eggs are not always fertile at that stage.

Lutino, blue and albino birds have been bred. Lutinos (yellow with red eyes) are golden yellow and have whitish wings. You also get green-yellow Alexandrines. The hereditary pattern of lutinos is the same as that for albinos (see p. 50), and the expectations for the blue variety is as for the blue mutation of the Black-masked Lovebird (see p. 117). Beware of some forms of abnormal plumage—this is not hereditary and after moulting, the plumage returns to its proper colour.

The Lutino-Alexandrine is canary
yellow with whitish wings.

African Ringneck Parrakeet (*P. krameri*) west Africa, Sudan, northern
Ethiopia, Pakistan, Bangladesh, India, Burma, south-east China and Sri
Lanka (illustrated p. 150)

Characteristics: 42 cm (16½ in) long. Male—green; the neckband begins at the
throat, where it is black, and joins the pink band at the nape; black stripe
from nostrils to eyes; beak red or black and red. Female—no neckband or
eye stripe. Young—as female; adult plumage appears at about two years.

The black stripe from the nostrils to the eyes makes this species easy to
distinguish from the Alexandrine. Africa has four races, and India two. This
is the only psittacine with such a wide distribution and the only representative
of the Parrakeet family in Africa. The Indian races are more frequently
imported than the African ones.

Housing and rearing: Ringnecks are reasonably easy to breed. The female
incubates her three or four eggs for twenty-four to twenty-six days, and the
youngsters leave the nest after about six weeks.

166

I know of a Budgerigar that reared a Ringneck, but it had to be fed by the breeder as well once it had left the nest.

Some Ringnecks are excellent talkers, repeating something like 100 words. of course, you can only expect this sort of success from a very young bird. Once tamed, the birds make very little use of their natural parrot voices. They produce the same mutations as the Alexandrines (illustrated p. 166).

Moustache Parrakeet (*P. alexandri*) Burma, Thailand, Vietnam, Hai-nan Toa Island, south China, Java and Borneo (illustrated p. 150)

Characteristics: 35 cm (13¾ in) long. Male—green; head greyish-blue with a black stripe from forehead to eyes; broad black stripe from underneath the beak to the ear coverts (the moustache); breast pink; upper mandible red, lower mandible black. Female—beak black, stronger pink on breast. Young—greener breast, turning pink after year; beak yellowish at first, later turning black or black and red.

Not many Moustache Parrakeets are ever offered for sale, so the price is naturally higher. Sexing is easy because of the different beak colours.
Housing and rearing: Although Moustache Parrakeets have shown themselves to be tameable in increasing numbers, and can learn to talk, they are really more suitable for keeping in the aviary. They have also been bred; the pair laid three eggs and the youngsters remained in the nest for five or six weeks.

Derbyan (*P. derbyana*) south-east Tibet, south-west China

Characteristics: 44 cm (17¼ in) long. Male—green; head greyish-blue with a black band from forehead to eyes; broad black stripe from underneath the lower mandible to below the ear coverts; belly bluish-pink; nape brilliant green; beak black until end of second year when upper mandible turns red. Female—black beak. Young—beak red at first, then black; achieves its final colour after two years. Full adult plumage in third year.
Housing and rearing: The Derbyan is rare and can hardly be considered a suitable subject for house rearing. The Chinese adore them. They can be tamed and taught to talk, but not very clearly.

They have been bred on a number of occasions; in 1933 in England and in 1963 for the first time in Germany. Three eggs were laid in the April and were incubated for twenty-eight days. The male often went into the nest to feed the female and young. The young left the nest after six or seven weeks. During breeding, the birds particularly enjoyed carrots, apples, soaked wheatmeal bread and dandelion leaves.

Derbyans are impervious to frost because they inhabit altitudes up to 3500 metres in their native land.

Plum-head/Blossom-headed Parrakeet (*P. cyanocephala*) India, southern China and Sri Lanka (illustrated p. 151)

Characteristics: 35 cm (13¾ in) long. Male—upperparts olive green; lower parts yellowish-green; head plum-coloured; black neck ring; blue-green band at the nape; brown shoulder patch; upper mandible orange, lower mandible blackish. Female—greyish-blue; neckband yellowish; no brown shoulder patch; upper mandible pale yellow, lower mandible dark grey. Young—as female. Adult plumage after two years.

Plum-heads are regularly available, but only in small numbers. They are not too expensive, but do cost more than Ringnecks. New imports are delicate, and have to be given time to get used to their new food. Plenty of variety in the diet and very careful observation are imperative.

You find both older and younger birds on sale, and it is very difficult to sex them under the age of two years because, until then, both male and female look alike. Not until a few red feathers appear in the head can you determine that the specimen is male.

Housing and rearing. In the house: I strongly recommend young Plum-heads for rearing in the house. They soon grow quiet and trusting and have a very pleasant twittering voice. They also learn to repeat a few words, but only when they are the only bird in the room.

It is possible to breed them in a bird room or in a cage that is at least 1.5 m (5 ft) long. The cage should be at eye level, in a quiet spot. Breeding usually succeeds best in a warm room because the breeding season falls in our winter and the birds rarely change over spontaneously to our summer. Therefore, you need to provide room temperature for breeding. They do not like a large nest box: a base of 17–20 cm (6¾–8 in) is sufficient with a depth of 30 cm (1 ft) and an entrance hole diameter of 5–6 cm (2–2¼ in) will be adequate. It is only the 22 cm (8¾ in) long tail that makes this bird look large. The male displays by running up and down a branch, twittering and bowing. The female lays four to six eggs and sits for twenty-two or twenty-three days. The youngsters leave the nest after about six weeks and are fed, mainly by the male, for some time afterwards. Sexing is only possible after the second moult.

Additional food: oats, soaked white bread, biscuits, chopped-up hard-boiled egg and greenfood.

In the garden: Plum-heads can be kept equally well in a flight with a frost-free shelter. They can tolerate a few degrees of frost but any more and their feet could be affected by frost.

Plum-heads are not destructive chewers; nor do they fight other birds. They get on well with Budgerigars, Elegant, Splendid and Redrump Parrakeets and many non-psittacine species.

Mutations: We know of a yellow mutation. The head remained reddish. There have also been reports of blue variations and birds with red patches.

Eclectus Parrots (*Eclectus*)

Grand Eclectus (*Lorius roratus*, 12 races) (illustrated p. 149)

Origin and habit: Moluccas, Ceram, Ambon, Sumba, Halmahera, Solomons, New Guinea and neighbouring islands, northern Queensland. Eclectus Parrots are found in the mountains and thickly wooded high jungles. Very little is known about their behaviour in the wild. On some of the South Sea Islands they favour the coconut plantations, which they use for food. They also raid the maize plantations and dig for tubers. The natives hunt them for food. They are not sociable and are only found in pairs during the breeding season. They breed in very tall, large hollow trees.

General remarks: In the past, Eclectus Parrots posed many questions for the scientists and aviculturists. They had been known about for almost a century before Dr A.B. Meyer, from the Munich Museum, was able to establish that the green bird was definitely the male and the red one was the female.

Despite improved transportation conditions, many of these Parrots arrive here in a delicate state of health. At first they refuse food and it is not always easy to get them to eat. Females are said to be even more delicate than males and, according to Heinroth, there are fewer of them in the wild. Prices vary greatly, but Eclectus Parrots have never been cheap.

These beautiful Parrots have very steady, quiet characters. They are not difficult to tame and even older birds respond to patient training. They only use their powerful beaks when they feel desperate. The male's voice is generally reserved for use during the breeding season, and resembles the cawing of a raven. The female's call is different; she occasionally lets out a kind of neighing laugh, usually when there is a sudden unexpected noise—the radio, the vacuum cleaner, and so on. Her other noises are very soft calls, not at all parrot-like. My Eclectus Parrot, named Papagena, can imitate a wide repertoire of words, some of which are clear, some of which are not.

Feeding: Fresh corn on the cob, boiled maize and rice in the early days, sunflower, various ripe fruit, carrots, rusk (also soaked), rose hips, hawthorn berries, rowan berries, grapes and chickweed, lettuce, dandelions and spinach.

Housing and rearing. In the house: Newly-imported birds must be kept at room temperature. I have had only good experiences with my Eclectus Parrots, unlike other authors. Although they are fruit-eaters by nature, they soon became accustomed to sunflower seed, so their droppings became firmer. Of course, you still have to offer them a variety of foods, especially if you want them to breed. Mine are in a cage measuring 115 cm (3 ft 9¼ in) long, 115 cm (3 ft 9¼ in) tall and 60 cm (2 ft) deep. The base is made from two drawers with high sides, to protect the room. I cover these with paper or sand, in rotation, because the birds need a sand bath at least once a week. I put a 5 cm (2 in) deep layer of sand on the bottom, and they also eat some of it because of the vital minerals it contains. In the wild they dig for roots in order to get these minerals. It is also important to provide a climbing branch, because they climb far more than they fly. They can use their beaks as a third leg to help them climb. I have found that a cage with a front that you can open completely is best as it is much easier to clean out, and to put a fresh branch inside. This will not bother them if you have taken the trouble to get them used to it slowly and quietly. You need heavy feeders that cannot be tipped over by the birds. They have a fairly high rate of water consumption, especially when eating plenty of sunflower seed or maize. A once-weekly spray with luke-warm water ensures a splendid plumage but keep them out of draughts or cool air immediately afterwards, and avoid spraying them in cold weather.

They become sexually mature at about four years old. The problem is really that they are loners outside the breeding season, and it is difficult to find a pair which actually get on with each other. It is the female who does all the courting, so on no account put two females with one male. Experiments with stuffed specimens have shown that a male will totally ignore another male, but a female hurls herself on to another female, intent upon murder.

They only lay two eggs. The female incubates alone for twenty-eight days. The male guards the entrance and spends the night in the box with her. Mine chose a box with a base 28×25 cm ($11 \times 9\frac{3}{4}$ in) with a depth of 45 cm (1 ft $5\frac{3}{4}$ in). The entrance hole was 10 cm (4 in) across. The eggs have to lie on a layer of woodshavings some 8 cm (3 in) thick, otherwise they can be crushed by the heavy birds. The eggs are 4.5 cm ($1\frac{3}{4}$ in) long and 3.3 cm ($1\frac{1}{3}$ in) wide, white and dull. The mating call of the male resembles a long drawn out 'miaou'. He then taps his beak against a branch or against the female's beak, making a sibilant noise all the time. However, it is the female who invites the actual mating. Sometimes she hangs from the roof of the cage. She also begs the male for food all the time and chases after him.

The young are naked for the first ten days, when dark down breaks through. They are completely covered in this thick down by the age of twenty-five days. The first feathers appear on the head and wings. It is then that you can tell the bird's sex. By eight weeks they have their full plumage and their colouring is identical to that of the parents, except for the colour of the beak and the iris. The red in a young female is somewhat darker and the tip of the upper mandible is still yellow. Not until they are about thirteen weeks old do they begin to feed themselves. I have reared thirteen youngsters. Two of my birds, hatched in 1973, reared young in the Bird Park at Metelen from 1976.

All these remarks also apply to the race *L. r. pectoralis.*

In the garden: New imports must be kept at room temperature. However, I have known well-acclimatized birds which overwintered without heating and

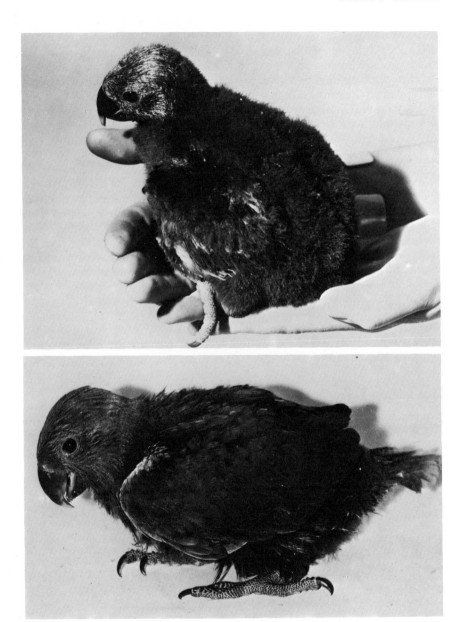

Top: Thirty-nine days old Eclectus Parrot. The red feathers in the head and wings have appeared. Bottom: The same bird aged seven weeks and two days.

came to no harm. They even went into the flight when it was frosty. They make very little use of their wings, even in the largest aviary. Instead, they much prefer climbing, and spend most of their time as high up as they can get. So, climbing trees and stout branches must be provided, otherwise they will spend all their time on the wire netting, which damages the tail feathers.

They do not gnaw very much; just supply them with fresh twigs. Strong wire netting is not necessary.

Red-sided Eclectus Parrot (*L. roratus pectoralis*) New Guinea and neighbouring islands (illustrated p. 171)

Characteristics: 39 cm (15¼ in) long. Male—green; flanks and underwings red; upper mandible orange to flesh coloured, lower mandible black; bend of wing pale blue; iris orange. Female—red; nape band, breast, belly and eye ring blue; tip of tail bright red; beak black; iris yellow. Young—can be sexed at four weeks, while still in the nest; complete plumage at eight weeks; remains a nestling for eleven weeks; independent after thirteen weeks; iris dark.

Vosmaeri's Eclectus Parrot (*L. roratus vosmaeri*) Moluccas, Halmahera and neighbouring islands

Characteristics: Female—as *L. r. pectoralis* but without the blue eye-ring; yellow border to tail.

Aru Islands Eclectus Parrot (*L. roratus aruensis*) Aru Islands

Characteristics: Female—as *L. r. pectoralis* but smaller; outer edge of flights slightly greenish.

Grand Eclectus Parrot (*L. roratus roratus*) Ceram, Ambon and south Moluccas

Characteristics: Female has violet belly; no blue eye-ring; undertail coverts yellow.

Riedel's Eclectus Parrot (*L. roratus riedeli*) Tenimber Islands

Characteristics: Female—completely red; broad, yellow tip to the tail (3 to 4 cm (1¼–1½ in)). Male—yellow edge to tail.

Cornelia's Eclectus Parrot (*L. roratus cornelia*) Sumba

Characteristics: Female—completely red; no yellow in the tail.

Index of parrot species

173

General index